PARANORMAL KENT

ROBERT BARD

AMBERLEY

First published 2024

Amberley Publishing
The Hill, Stroud
Gloucestershire, GL5 4EP

www.amberley-books.com

British Library Cataloguing in Publication Data.
A catalogue record for this book is available from the British Library.

ISBN 978 1 3981 0802 8 (print)
ISBN 978 1 3981 0803 5 (ebook)

Typesetting by SJmagic DESIGN SERVICES, India.
Printed in Great Britain.

Contents

Introduction

Paranormal Kent is my second book on the paranormal, following *Paranormal Berkshire*. As a professional historian blessed with a large amount of scepticism and cynicism, I find researching the paranormal fascinating because one is always dealing with subjective evidence – is the witness reliable? Could the event be due to ordinary causes? Is the event merely a product of repetition – a grey lady is seen here or there and over time becomes a legend? When researching *Paranormal Berkshire* one of the most interesting incidents that I came across related to some very unusual sightings – creatures that we would regard as mythological but somehow seem to make it into the real world. According to two eyewitness reports at both Windsor, alongside the Thames, and further along the river at Boulters Lock near Maidenhead, a 'non-standard' wolf-like creature was spotted, observed very closely, followed, and recorded in two separate police reports. The witnesses in both cases were on-duty policemen, and women. I, like most rational people, have never believed in the existence of werewolves, but it made me wonder what exactly the creature was – what could they have really seen? In looking at the paranormal-rich county of Kent, I decided to include similar cryptid sightings and a 'time-slip' incident in Tonbridge where a person unwittingly stepped back in time for a few minutes. In the writing of this book, I was determined to visit most of the sites myself to experience the atmosphere; to try and get a feel for the reports, and where possible talk to eyewitnesses. As with the writing of my previous paranormal book, I developed a habit of asking friends and acquaintances if they had ever seen a ghost. One friend mentioned a weekend stay at Coombe Abbey in Oxfordshire where she said she'd seen and photographed the face of a monk in her bedroom after feeling a presence. I include it simply because it summarises the dilemma of 'what are we really seeing?'

A well-publicised ghost, or mysterious figure, which appeared in a photo taken at the ruins of Eynsford Castle led me to contacting Alan Tigwell, a respected researcher of the paranormal, in particular in relation to sites in Kent. I asked him a number of questions about both the Eynsford Castle figure and a number of other incidents he had investigated which he answered, in my opinion, very honestly and I have included in this book.

A listing of paranormal events in Kent is available on the comprehensive https://paranormaldatabase.com, but the events I have chosen for this book are in my opinion interesting, often plausible, and at the very least make an open-minded sceptic like myself pause for thought.

Coombe Abbey image of a face, 2014. (Courtesy of Sylva Konvalinka Le Boeuf)

Bidborough, Royal Tunbridge Wells

The ancient church of St Lawrence is in Bidborough High Street and is well worth a visit. The village has a population of under 1,000 and is just north of Tunbridge Wells. Parts of the church of St Lawrence date back to the tenth century, and during the twelfth century the building was extended. I visited on a sunny summers' day and felt the prominent church had a brooding presence. In July 1998, in the vicinity of the church two visitors observed three phantom monks floating rapidly down the pathway This, not surprisingly, left the visitors stunned and they hastily departed the churchyard. Neil Arnold, author of a number of Kent-based paranormal works, reports that 'they noticed that the hooded figures had a strange hue about them – particularly under their cowls, where their faces should have been'.[1] There are two possible areas where the siting occurred as there are two pathways leading up to the church.

In July 1998, in the vicinity of the church two visitors observed three phantom monks floating rapidly down the pathway.

1. Arnold, Neil, *Haunted Tunbridge Wells* (The History Press – Kindle edition), p.13.

Brenchley, Tonbridge

All Saints at Brenchley has an extensive churchyard and feels anything but creepy or spooky. The atmosphere is quiet and restful with lovely views over the surrounding countryside. The day I visited the weather was sunny and warm. The reported ghost here is that of a Roman soldier.

During the summer of 1988 a man visited the churchyard and was reading tombstone inscriptions when he felt a presence nearby. He looked up and was startled to see the head and shoulders of a Roman soldier. He reported that the figure wore a 'close-fitting helmet', and 'looked young and fair of face'. The spectre appeared to be staring at a gravestone. However, when the witness approached, the figure, like so many ghosts, disappeared.

All Saints at Brenchley. The ghostly Roman soldier is described as wearing a 'close-fitting helmet', and looking 'young and fair of face'.

In the summer of 1988, the spectre of a Roman soldier materialised and appeared to be staring at a gravestone.

Challock, Ashford

A strange creature has been reported in and around the village, notably in the area of the fourteenth-century St Cosmas & St Damian's Church. The area is wooded, gloomy and the lanes between the church and the village are tree lined. 'Local residents' recount sightings of a strange animal which follows at a distance and seems to resemble a huge goat with glowing amber eyes and horns. It also has a bearded face!

It has been reported that 'animals are discovered in the woods, torn apart and strewn across the ground'. This might be more indicative of a large wild cat than a paranormal beast. A black and white photograph of the creature exists online and is not, in my opinion particularly convincing. It shows two distant lights surrounded by darkness. Kenton Bowmann, writing in 2017,[2] commented that 'the beast was often

A grey presence and heavy crashing noises have been reported around the church. (Photo Kent Online)

---

2. ghostsnghouls.com/gray-beast-of-challock.

seen in the 1930s and has made more appearances in the new millennium. A young man once tracked the beast for several hundred yards before it turned on him with such force that the young man could do nothing but run for his life. Arriving back at the church, he locked himself in and immediately passed out from fear, only to awake the next morning, safe and snug in his car. Who took him there and how they entered the bolted church door is still not known to this day'.

Recent reports from the area around the church speak of heavy crashing noises coming from the dense undergrowth and a strange, sickly smoke-like smell following behind people as they hike through the woods. A grey 'presence' is often mentioned, caught in a slight sideways glance. It is thought that the village was moved to its present location at the time of the plague, although some say that the prevalence of witchcraft in the area made only the church a safe place to visit, and then only by day when a priest was in attendance.

Cranbrook, nr Sissinghurst

St Dunstan's, known as 'the Cathedral of the Weald', is a large and architecturally interesting church. Above the south porch there was once a room known as 'Baker's Jail' or 'Baker's Hole'. John Baker (1488–1558) was an early Chancellor of the Exchequer. He was also known as the 'Bloody Baker' due to his brutal prosecution of Protestants. Supposedly, the groans of the prisoners who were held here can still be heard. However, Paranormal investigator Charles Igglesden is sceptical of such claims, commenting, 'I'm afraid it's only rats; but there is nothing like a weird tradition of this sort. It helps you a lot in telling this story.'

Supposedly one can hear the screams of the infuriated mob burning Sir John Baker alive in the market place but as Sir John died of an illness in his bed so this is unlikely. He is buried in the churchyard and has a memorial in the knave.

THE SOUTH PORCH

This porch was built about 1390. The wooden door was added in 1569. It cost 17 shillings and 7 pence - less than £1 at the time, but that's more than £2,000 in today's money. Look up at the ceiling. You will see a stone-carved Green Man.

If you look at the porch from outside you will see it has two storeys. The room above is called a parvise. It was built as the Vicar's vestry: steps go up to it inside the church. But it also once served a grimmer purpose. Its Cranbrook nickname is 'Baker's Jail'. Sir John Baker of Sissinghurst was the local magistrate during the reign of Mary Tudor (1553-58). It is said he imprisoned a protestant prisoner here: we know for sure the man was taken to Maidstone to be burned, one of several local martyrs.

The south porch information board, Brenchley.

The steps inside the church next to the porch that led up to the reputedly haunted imprisonment area.

The impressive Baker family monument.

John Baker (1488–1588), who served as the Chancellor of the Exchequer, was also known as the 'Bloody Baker' due to his brutal prosecution of Protestants.

Blue Bell Hill, Chatham

On the late September day I visited Blue Bell Hill it was cold, windy and atmospheric, with views stretching way into the distance. It is easy to imagine the area being associated with the paranormal, particularly in the light of a large haunting memorial commemorating three men who died nearby in an air ambulance crash.

Blue Bell Hill is possibly one of the most haunted roads in England with over fifty reported ghostly sightings in the past century. At the top of the hill until fairly recently stood the Upper Bell Inn, fringed by shrub woodland where a butcher murdered a young man in a field. The body was found just inside the wood. The ghost of the murderer has been allegedly seen near the scene of his crime. As is often the way with ghostly legends, names are attributed to the phantoms. In this case the victim became known as 'the Blue Boy' and the alleged scene of the murder, 'Blue Boy Field'.

The late Peter Underwood (*Ghosts of Kent*) summed up the Blue Bell Hill ghost phenomena quite well when he observed that 'stories, invariably second- or third-hand, tell of someone being picked up and given a lift home; on arrival they have disappeared and when the person giving the lift goes to the house to tell the people there what has happened, he or she is told that the person they gave a lift to died, at the spot where they picked up the "ghost", some months or years ago ... I have yet to locate an authentic and first-hand incident.' Having said this, there are some interesting reports. The following are just some of the alleged sightings.

In 1934, a young woman, Renee, was riding her bicycle home on a dim autumn evening. When travelling down the hill, out of nowhere a dark mist appeared before her, which she hit. Renee was thrown to the ground. On looking around there was nothing to explain why she had fallen. In the same year a man saw a young woman standing in the middle of the road. Concerned, he pulled over and offered her a lift. The girl asked to be taken to Church Street close to the cemetery. Despite it being out of his way, he agreed and took her to her destination. Turning around to speak to her as he reached Church Street. the gentleman was shocked to discover his passenger had disappeared into thin air.

In December 1967, *The Kent Messenger* reported the strange tale of a man and his friend travelling home late at night. As they passed the bus stop at the foot of the hill, they saw a young woman standing alone. Realising that the last bus had long gone, they pulled over and offered her a lift. The young woman accepted and climbed into the back seat. She gave her address and the car travelled on. When they arrived at the address, the two men were astonished to discover that their passenger was no longer in the car. When they made enquiries at the house they were told that it was once the home of a young woman killed a few years earlier on Blue Bell Hill in a tragic car accident.

In the winter of 1968, a gentleman pushing his bicycle up a steep section of the hill was stunned to see a young woman emerge from the trees at the side of the road in a flimsy cotton dress. The woman appeared distressed. After he passed her, he glanced back over his shoulder out of curiosity, but she had disappeared. In November 1965, four young women were travelling home from a hen night. The driver of the car, Suzanne Browne, was to be married the next day to RAF technician Brian Wetton. As the four travelled on to Blue Bell Hill, Suzanne lost control of the car and crashed head on with a Jaguar heading in the opposite direction. One young woman died immediately; Suzanne and another of her friends died later in hospital. Soon after there were sightings of a ghostly woman. Another similar incident occurred on a rainy night when a gentleman returning home from his late shift at a local paper mill took pity on a young woman standing drenched at a bus stop. Once again, the young woman accepted a lift and climbed into the back seat of the vehicle. By the time they reached her home, she had disappeared into thin air. At around the same time, an astonished lorry driver called into a local café for a strong cup of tea to steady his nerves. He reported that he had agreed to give a girl a lift to a nearby village. She climbed into his cab, before disappearing into thin air a few minutes later. In 1971, a young man called James Skene was driving home when a woman suddenly appeared in front of his car. Braking quickly, he offered to take the woman home. Once again she disappeared before they reached their destination.

On 7 November 1992, Ian Sharpe was driving on Blue Bell Hill. A woman wearing light-coloured clothes suddenly appeared in front of his car. Unable to brake in time, he hit the woman and immediately stopped. Climbing out of his car, he was shocked to discover that the woman was nowhere to be found. He drove to the nearest police station to report the incident.

On a dark, late November evening in 1992 Chris Dawkins was driving on Blue Bell Hill when out of nowhere, a woman wearing a red headscarf dashed in front of the car. He felt her hit the bonnet. Shaking, he got out of the car but couldn't find the woman. Frightened that the woman may be trapped under his vehicle, he summoned his father and the police. Despite an extensive search, they also failed to find any sign of the woman.

The parking area at the top of the hill provides spectacular views over the surrounding countryside.

Right: A sombre, sad and haunting memorial commemorating three men of the Kent Air Ambulance who perished when their helicopter crashed nearby on Sunday 26 July 1998.

Below: The view from the top of the hill is spectacular and adds to the isolation and loneliness of the area.

Believing that he had hit a woman, a motorist climbed out of his car and was shocked to discover she was nowhere to be found.

Chatham Dockyard

On the day of my visit with an enthusiastic friend we realised that the sheer size of the dockyard warranted a whole day rather than the planned couple of hours. The dockyard is well organised and there are tours and cafeterias. It also boasts numerous paranormal entities, and was one of the sites chosen by the *Most Haunted* team. Paranormal reports date back to the time of Samuel Pepys, English diarist and naval administrator who wrote of his official visit to the dockyard in 1661:

> Then to the Hill House at Chatham, where I never was before, and I found a pretty pleasant house, and am pleased with the armes that hang up there. Here we supped very merry, and late to bed; Sir William telling me that old Edge-barrow, his predecessor, did die and walk in my chamber, did make me somewhat afraid, but not so much as for mirth's sake I did seem. So to bed in the Treasurer's chamber. Lay and slept till three in the morning, and then waking and by the light of the moon I saw my pillow (which overnight I flung from me) stand upright, but not bethinking myself what it might be I was a little afraid, but sleep overcome all, and so lay till nigh morning, at which time I had a candle brought me, and a good fire made, and in general it was a great pleasure all the time I staid here to see how I am respected and honoured by all people …

Neil Arnold, author of *Haunted Chatham*, relates that when he was a child in the 1970s and early 1980s, both his father and grandfather had worked at the 80-acre Historic Dockyard. He recounts a particular story of when his father was in the rest room 'getting his head down'. The door to the room was ajar, and through the crack his father could see the figure of an old man peering back at him. The man wore similar overalls, but his father was not familiar with the man as being on the same shift, and he sensed that there was something unusual and 'old-fashioned' about him. This was confirmed when the man very slowly began to fade away until he no longer stood in the doorway. Another employee in the room Arnold mentioned saw his father slowly sit up and gaze towards the door, but they did not discuss what he had seen. His father felt no malevolence from the phantom and the next day, whilst making a cup of tea, he was approached by the other worker, who said that he had also seen the figure in the overalls vanish into thin air. He tells another story, this time of a worker asked to clear out one of the rooms which was packed full of old junk and had become choked with weeds. Upon entering the room both men shouted in horror as a black, phantasmal creature came rushing past them out of the door. One of the witnesses stated categorically that the 'animal' had not been a domestic cat or fox, but something 'far larger which moved at lightning speed'.

The dockyard has the fifth most haunted house in Britain, the Commissioner's House. A duty manager who conducted walks saw a young girl in her early teens standing on the lawn who then proceeded to disappear through the gate out of the garden. In 1961, one of the first ever ghost hunts was conducted at the Drill Hall, Dock Road. It was reported in the *Chatham Standard* of 31 October, in an article by Frederick Sanders, that at midnight on Friday 20 October a light flickered in the clock tower and went out; the mechanism ceased to function and the hands remained stationary. During the following week several attempts were made to get the clock to go. For a few hours it worked well, and then at various times, from 5.25 p.m. to 8.45 p.m., it would immobilise itself. There was nothing mechanically wrong with the ex-Royal Marine barracks' clock. The clock tower was formerly the Royal Naval storehouse. Sanders writes that on the night of Friday 27th, he had strolled away from the barracks and was turning round at the top of the hill leading down to Pembroke naval barracks when a hatless and very distraught young sailor stopped him and asked for a match to light a cigarette, which he held in trembling fingers. He remarked to him that as he was coming past the deserted Royal Marine barracks he had stopped to look through the gates to see what the time was by the clock in the tower, when suddenly he caught the faraway sound of marching feet. Nearer and nearer came the steady tramp, tramp, tramping. Then, before his startled gaze appeared the band of the Royal Marines followed by a standard bearer, behind whom marched a squad of marines with fixed bayonets! He brought to the notice of the gentleman in blue that if the squad was really a 'ghost squad' he would not have heard them, but only seen them. He told Sanders that he'd seen them and heard them, and he knew they were ghosts of Royal Marines because though the band was playing, no martial music filled the midnight air. Mumbling his thanks for the light, he lurched away, and with a sharp, weird cry ran down the hill towards HMS Pembroke.

Underwood speaks of the ghostly sound of limping footsteps, and the 'tapping of a crutch or wooden leg' in the vicinity of St Mary's Barracks. The ghost is meant to be that of an ex-serviceman who was shot after being mistaken for an intruder. Underwood states that, 'The sounds have most frequently been reported during the Middle Watch, midnight to 4 a.m., when, it might be thought, the night is at its darkest, shadows can easily assume physical forms and mistakes can easily happen.' Although the ghost may be nothing more than the product of an overactive imagination, it has acquired a name over the years – Peg-Leg Jack. He has also been heard towards Room 34 of Cumberland Block, said to be the oldest part of the barracks.

A story appeared in *The Telegraph* on 18 February 2010 concerning the ropery, which is probably the longest brick building in the world. Fred had worked at the ropery for almost fifty years. He experienced a few ghost encounters according to the newspapers. 'Sometimes it can feel a bit funny, especially when you are switching the lights off at night. Each light has to be switched off individually and, as you were walking along, and hear people behind you … the ropery is also said to be haunted by a handful of bobbing boys – children dressed in tatty attire dating back a couple of centuries.' In September 2011, one of the security guards at the dockyard mentioned that whilst working late one night in the ropery, he'd been spooked by the sound of footsteps when there was no one else in the building. Members of the public whilst visiting the mast house reported excruciating pains in their heads when standing almost on the exact spot where an alleged murder took place in 1875. On 16 April 1875 at 3.00 p.m., two men were working on a mast. One of the men was shaping

The clock tower in the dockyard was, according to researcher Frederick Sanders, haunted. 'The light in the tower flickered and went out; the mechanism ceased to function ...'

Commissioner's Residence, one of the country's most haunted buildings, where one of the resident ghosts had allegedly hanged herself in one of the large Georgian star windows that front the river.

Above: A horrified sailor reported the peculiar sounds of marching men and seeing a phantom parade.

Left: The mast house has retained the feelings from a murder that occurred here in 1875.

Right: The ropery area to the right, where children dressed in tatty attire dating back a couple of centuries have been seen.

Below: In September 2011, one of the security guards mentioned that whilst working late one night in the ropery, he'd been spooked by the sound of footsteps when there was no one else in the building.

the timbers, and the other was watching him. The onlooker, who was in possession of a pickaxe-type tool, struck the other man across the head, resulting in death. It is possible that the mast house has retained the feelings from the murder that occurred in 1875.[3]

3. Arnold, Neil, *Haunted Chatham* (The History Press).

Canterbury Cathedral

The cathedral is the pilgrimage destination of Thomas Becket, Archbishop of Canterbury from 1161 to 1170. Becket was murdered in the most gruesome manner imaginable.

Due to some later regretted unfortunate words uttered by Becket's former friend Henry II, four of Henry's knights went to arrest Becket. An early account tells us that Becket held tight onto one of the cathedral's pillars to prevent them seizing him, then one of the knights brought his sword down on Becket's head, slicing off his crown. Two of the other knights then started to attack Becket and the third blow killed the archbishop. It is recorded that they cracked open his skull, spilling his brains onto the cathedral floor! Underwood comments that the inevitable ghost of Thomas Becket, which was near one of the pillars in the crypt, was 'distinct and unmistakable'. He continues: 'I have another report of a shadowy figure that could not be explained, being seen by a group of visitors to the cathedral. At first, they thought someone must be rehearsing for a play or tableau of some kind for the costume was unmistakably of olden days but they discovered, on enquiry, that such was not the case and the figure disappeared in circumstances that were quite inexplicable. One of the cathedral staff was very interested in the experiences of this group and told them that he had heard about a similar sighting a few months earlier.' The atmosphere and overwhelming sense of history and tragedy that pervades Canterbury Cathedral could well influence certain individuals, but could it account for a figure seen by two different groups of people on two different occasions?

Unsurprisingly one of the cathedral ghosts is that of a monk which has been spotted in the area and has been reported to wander about the cloisters.

Almost as if to verify that the cathedral has its resident phantoms, a visitor wrote on a paranormal website: 'I was recently looking over some photos I had taken back in 2011 of Canterbury Cathedral and surrounding precincts and was disappointed at how dark they were, so I decided to apply the 'autofix' function of Windows Photo Gallery to see if they would lighten up anymore. I was then quite surprised at what I saw in one photograph. I've attached the original unaltered photograph, the 'autofixed' version, and a zoom into the area of interest. Apparently, there is a 'legend' of a bricked-up nun that haunts the area in the vicinity of the cloisters, but a ghostly monk has also been seen flitting around there – do you think it looks male or female? I can't decide!' https://ghostsnghouls.com/ghost-photo-canterbury-cathedral/

A passage called the 'Dark Entry' is thought to be haunted by the ghost of Nell Cook, who was once a servant of one of the cathedral's canons. The person who she was working for was having an affair, which sent Cook into a rage. She decided to get back at her employer by poisoning some of his food. Not only did the tainted food kill the canon, but it also took the life of his lover. Cook was buried alive beneath the Dark Entry as a punishment. It is believed that it is her ghost that haunts the passageway,

Could the marked image be the phantom of a bricked-up nun that haunts the area in the vicinity of the cloisters. (Photo: https://ghostsnghouls.com/ghost-photo-canterbury-cathedral)

The phantom of the figure of a nun and the ghost of Simon of Sudbury are reported to have been seen.

The ghost of a monk has been spotted in the area and has been reported to wander about the cloisters of the cathedral.

where for some unknown reason, she is mostly spotted on Friday evenings. The legend attached to this tale is that anyone who catches sight of Nell Cook's ghost is said to perish soon after the encounter. If you believe in superstitions, it makes one think twice before visiting the passageway area of this cathedral.

These are the standard cathedral ghost stories. Probably of more interest is a letter received by the late paranormal investigator Peter Underwood in 1977 from a Mr C. J. Fleetney of Canterbury who was involved with the cathedral. Fleetney's letter read as follows:

As a trainee Reader, Lay-Minister of the Church of England, shortly to be admitted to the Office, I was expected to attend a series of lectures on ministering to the dying. The venue was the Chapel of Our Lady Undercroft, in the crypt of Canterbury Cathedral. The evening of Thursday, 19 October 1976, was dark. The clouds were low and racing across the sky from the south-west, driven by a gale that was fast stripping the last of the autumn leaves from the trees. My wife and I parked our car some way from the cathedral and leaned into the wind and bitter rain as we made our way along St Margaret's Street, across St Peter's Street, and through narrow Mercery Lane towards Christ Church Gate. There were few people about and, it seemed, no vehicles, and the only noise was the booming of the gale, the creaking of the swinging signs above shop fronts, and the hiss of the rain on the pavements. The cathedral, vast and grey, towered above us into the blackness of the night. The south porch, the main entrance, was closed and gated, and not a trace of light glimmered from the nave windows. In company with other people we made our way across the wet turf to the tiny, narrow door set in the wall of the south-west transept. One or two small electric lights threw vague shadows among the tattered battle flags stirring in the wind, in St Michael's Chapel. The great building stretched away in deep shadow, hinting at enormous height and space. High above us, in the fan vaulting of the central tower, the gale boomed and muttered. We followed a verger down, under the south aisle of the choir, to the crypt. Part of the Chapel of Our Lady Undercroft is frequently used as a lecture hall, the low-pitched nave, and the lecturer uses a lectern in a central position, with his back to the altar. The entire chapel is on one level; there are no steps to chancel or sanctuary. It is the oldest part of the cathedral, having survived the fires that destroyed the building above during the early Middle Ages. The chapel is not an ideal lecture hall as it is necessarily cluttered by short heavy Norman columns which support the tremendous weight above. 'The chapel was well-lighted and warm, comfortably full, but we managed to find seats in the centre but to the right of the speaker. A verger sat at the controls of the public address system and those of us who were students settled down with pen and pad to take notes as the lecture progressed, while the greater number, my wife included, enjoyed listening to this man, well-known in his particular field. Beyond the lecturer the chancel and sanctuary was in semi-darkness illuminated only by the light from the main body of the chapel. From where we were sitting the altar was obscured by a column, and when I glanced up from my notes, my view beyond the lecturer was the curving blind arcading of the wall between the altar and the corner of the organ which in turn obscured my view to the extreme left. Above the wall's blind arcading the narrow lancets soared up to break ground level. They were clear glass and the gale caused the shadows of bare branches to toss and flicker across the lattice-work. Some ten minutes before the mid-lecture break I was aware of a flicker of movement against the blind arcading, some thirty feet from where I was sitting. I glanced quickly from my notes and saw the movement again. I realised that I had caught a brief glimpse of a verger moving from left to right: that is, from the point where the corner of the organ blocked my view, towards the altar, masked by the column close to my chair. Once again, just before the lecturer closed the first part of his talk, I caught this flicker of movement as the figure moved along the arcading towards the altar. The recess lasted some ten minutes and as question time was to follow people were scribbling notes on small squares of paper given out for the purpose. I asked my wife whether she had noticed the verger moving about, beyond the lecturer. She said that she had noticed movement, but not at pavement level, rather higher up, near the windows. While we spoke, she drew my attention suddenly to a movement. Together we agreed that in fact she could see the shadows of the wind-tossed branches, and perhaps the shadows of people walking round the Corona towards the King's School. I suggested that in fact it was a poor time to prepare the altar for the next day's services, as the constant movement was, to say the least, disturbing when one was feverishly taking notes. The lecturer called us to order and question time began. I kept my eyes half trained on the distant wall at first but quickly became immersed in the discussion. Then, suddenly, there he was again! Moving towards the altar, close to the arcading. I turned to my notes, mildly annoyed. A few minutes later, due to a remark by the lecturer, I glanced up and experienced an indescribable and overwhelming fear that welled up inside me and I saw the figure move in a ghastly kind of puppet-like motion from right to left, along the arcading, and then vanish behind the organ. In that instant I somehow knew that the cassocked figure I was seeing was somehow unreal. I waited for it to return, left to right, but true to form it did not appear while I waited, and before I could relax and turn my attention to the lecturer, the session ended. The lecture was followed by tea and cakes. We milled around and people formed small groups to discuss the theme of the evening. I waited my opportunity and waylaid the busy verger. 'Were you busy preparing vestments for tomorrow's services just now?' I asked. 'I've been at the public address console all evening, Sir, why?' He was attempting to edge past me anxious to get things cleared away, for it was late and no doubt he had a full day facing him on the Friday. 'Oh, I thought I saw you or one of your colleagues ...' I saw him searching my face. 'I'm the only verger on duty tonight, but you thought you saw someone over by the far wall?' He pointed towards the far wall between the altar and the organ. I nodded and the verger eased me to one side and smiled. 'I'm the only verger here tonight, Sir,' he repeated. 'Now, if you'll excuse me.' It was quite obvious that he had no intention of discussing something that he knew well enough I had seen. 'I did not question anyone else that evening. I ought to have done, but things drifted on and we broke up and went our separate ways. Several days later I mentioned the incident to one of the Cathedral guides. She considered for a moment but said that apart from the well-known 'Becket's Shadow' which can be seen on one of the crypt columns, she knew of no other 'ghost' in the Undercroft. The facts are that at no time did I see the figure when I actually watched for it. It only appeared when I became involved with my notes and glanced up, briefly. At first it was just a flicker of black against the stone of the arcading. Later it seemed to be a thin person of medium height wearing a cassock. I do not recall head or hands, just a cassock, drifting along in a busy, purposeful manner. It was not until I saw it move from right to left that I realised I had seen it move, perhaps five times, always from left to right Only on the last occasion did its behaviour strike me as somehow horrible and extremely frightening; only then said that apart from the well-known 'Becket's Shadow' which can be seen on one of the crypt columns, she knew of no other 'ghost' in the Undercroft. The facts are that at no time did I see the figure when I actually watched for it. It only appeared when I became involved with my notes and glanced up, briefly. At first it was just a flicker of black against the stone of the arcading. Later it seemed to be a thin person of medium height wearing a cassock. I do not recall head or hands, just a cassock, drifting along in a busy, purposeful manner. It was not until I saw it move from right to left that I realised I had seen it move, perhaps five times, always from left to right Only on the last occasion did its behaviour strike me as somehow horrible and extremely frightening; only then did it strike me that it might be other than a verger ...

Sudbury Tower, Canterbury

Simon of Sudbury (1317–81), an unpopular Archbishop of Canterbury, was a victim of Wat Tyler's Peasants' Revolt and was seized by the mob from a chapel in the Tower of London, and dragged across to nearby Tower Hill, where he was summarily beheaded with a blunt sword. His head is now in a cabinet in the vestry of St Gregory's Church in Sudbury, Suffolk. I was allowed to examine the skull on a visit to the church several years ago and the sword hack marks are clearly visible on the back of the skull. Sudbury's headless body is buried in Canterbury Cathedral. Curiously, a lead cannonball has been put in place of his missing head.

Sudbury's ghost has more frequently been reported to haunt the tower a short distance away that bears his name. Peter Underwood stated that 'a possible reason might be that his head and his body were never reunited; yet the figure that is thought to be the ghost of Simon of Sudbury is a tall and dignified man with a grey beard and

The tower haunted by Simon of Sudbury, who is seen as but a tall and dignified man with a grey beard and a fresh complexion.

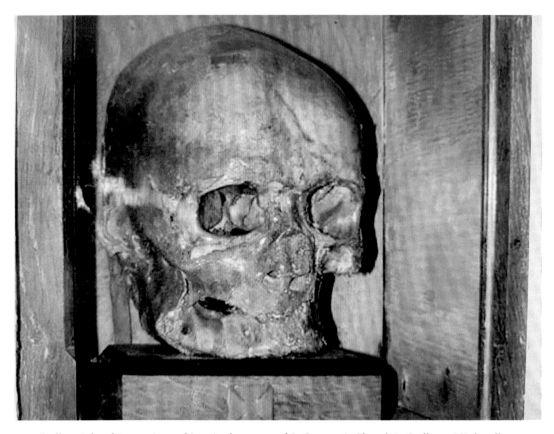

Sudbury's head is now in a cabinet in the vestry of St Gregory's Church in Sudbury. His headless body is buried in Canterbury Cathedral.

a fresh complexion'. Underwood writes, 'Eighty-year-old Charles Denne told me that he had dwelled there with a ghost for over twenty years. It all began when he retired one evening to his bedroom at the top of the Sudbury Tower, where he lived all alone. After a busy day repairing, strange tapping noises were heard, which sometimes came before he had the feeling that his "visitor" was in the room with him'.[4]

---

4. Underwood, Peter, *Ghosts of Kent: Illustrated Edition.*

Tiny Tim's Tearoom, Canterbury

Workmen working on restoring the building during the 2000s reported the sounds of children playing on the staircase, strange noises in the attic, and youngsters whispering in a panelled room where they had found the relics from several children.

During restoration works in the early 2000s the mummified bodies of three children were discovered in the attic of the building.

Chartwell, Westerham

Now a National Trust property, Chartwell was for forty years the home of Winston Churchill. Not surprisingly he has been seen here, as Robin Fedden recounts in his *Churchill and Chartwell* (1968). Researcher Peter Underwood says that his own enquiries 'support the generally accepted idea that the studio in the garden, where he [Churchill] was perhaps more relaxed than anywhere else, where some of his paintings adorn the walls, and where he spent so many happy hours, is probably more haunted than any other part of the place'. He further repeats an incident in which Randolph, Sir Winston's only son, 'described one occasion when he distinctly saw his dead father

The studio in the grounds, where Churchill's ghost has been seen.

Randolph, Sir Winston's only son, described one occasion when he talked to his dead father in the house.

in the room where a white marble bust of Lady Churchill stands near an old leather armchair. Randolph saw his father sitting in this armchair and, he always claimed, had a long discussion with him concerning men and events and the dangers that had overtaken the world since Sir Winston had died in 1965.'[5]

5. Underwood, *Peter, Ghosts of Kent: Illustrated Edition*, p. 223.

Chilham (between Ashford and Canterbury)

Chilham is a stunningly beautiful, slightly out of the way ancient village. In researching this book it was probably the prettiest and most unexpected gem I visited. A part of unspoiled old-world England, it lays claim to at least three phantoms.

Chilham Castle lies off the village square. It is privately owned and as of April 2021 was for sale. The bar in the castle is rumoured to be haunted by an unknown girl who has been seen by staff. An old story has it that she was bricked up alive by a previous owner of the castle, for reasons unknown.

The White Horse in the village square dates from 1422. In 1956, two complete and perfectly preserved male skeletons were found under the kitchen floor at a depth of 2 feet. They were possibly soldiers killed during the Wat Tyler rebellion, in 1381.

Chilham Castle. The bar area is haunted by an unknown girl who has been seen by staff.

The entrance gatehouse to Chilham Castle in the village square.

The White Horse. Two long-dead soldiers have haunted the pub, reported to be dressed in tattered uniforms.

The White Horse. In 1956, two complete and perfectly preserved male skeletons were found under the kitchen floor.

The skeletons were buried in the churchyard of St Mary's, Chilham, after a coroner's inquest said they were ancient bones and not the result of undetected crime. The two dead soldiers have allegedly haunted the pub, reported to be dressed in tattered uniforms. Their manifestation is accompanied by the sounds of creaking leather. The ghost of an elderly man in clerical clothing has been seen standing at the fireplace, his hands clasped behind his back, reputedly at ten o'clock every morning. Furthermore, a former vicar who committed suicide here is believed to make appearances.

Fort Amherst, Chatham

I visited Fort Amherst on a sunny autumn afternoon in 2021 and found the fort tunnels to be closed. My ghost-hunting travel companion (Glenn Robinson) talked to some gentlemen seated outside the nearby cafeteria who arranged for us to be given a guided tour with numerous anecdotes of their own ghostly experiences and where they happened. Fort Amherst, it seems, has a high ghost per square foot density. The tunnels are extensive and there are frequent organised ghost hunts taking place. The ghost-hunt team gave us an extensive tour of the tunnels and related a large number of paranormal events they had personally witnessed. I failed to witness anything myself, but the experiences related were convincing.

Susie Higgins and her partner Mark Gower investigated Fort Amherst a few years ago. Susie told author and ghost hunter Neil Arnold in 2011 what happened: 'Two incidents that stick in our minds took place at the Guard/Gate House. The building is on the far side of the grounds, opposite the tunnels. You descend down stone steps and under an arch which connects a similar building that has a dead end road running through the middle. You then enter a two-storey stone building which has a musty smell and large metal beds that protrude within the rooms. The ground floor has white curved ceilings with peeling paint. On the first floor are three two-bedded rooms which have big heavy damp mattresses stuffed with straw. Each room has an old fireplace with a fire basket and grate. It is a very foreboding building. On their first occasion, by torchlight, we were led through with a group of other people, but we were at the back and as the people in front had moved along a lot quicker, we were left walking the first-floor corridor past the bedrooms. There was a distinct atmosphere of being followed and a feeling of dread, as you would feel if someone was walking close by behind you and was about to charge at you. This feeling became so intense and angry that we literally scrambled to get out of the corridor and up the stone steps outside to the grass level, and only then could we look behind us. This building has an alleged spirit the resident medium calls "The Master", who allegedly attacks [the Medium] by dragging him out and slashing at his back. As a group we did witness him being "attacked", which prompted two of the volunteer security staff to help him out of the building where he lifted his shirt and, for all to see, he had long fresh scratch marks on his back. There is definitely something festering in there but I would suggest it is just an angry spirit. The second incident, a year later, we were back in the Guard/Gate House nearing the end of a paranormal investigation with Amherst's staff. This time each bedroom on the first floor individually held groups of people. In our room alone there were nine. A trigger alarm was set up in the corridor. Mark, my daughter Charlotte, and I were sitting on a low wooden bench with the beds to our left and other people, including a friend of ours named David, were sitting on them. In front of us was one of the volunteer helpers standing with his head just under a high-level shelf. We were in semi-darkness, and I started to goad the nasty spirit that allegedly haunts the building. We could hear a knocking sound, similar to a piece of wood being hit against the wooden doors to each bedroom/bay. The atmosphere changed dramatically, and several people commented on how uneasy they felt. Suddenly five of us witnessed a dark solid shadow form from the floor in front of the volunteer and slowly – this shadow became 6ft, then 7ft – grow up the wall to the ceiling. As soon as it did so, it shot out left and across two people sitting on a bed, which made them jump and scream as they felt the pressure of it, then the shadow seemed to become black liquid off the bed, swoosh past us, which made us sit right back to let it pass, and then it disappeared through the closed door, setting the trigger alarm off. Some people were visibly shaken and I have to say it left us speechless. The volunteer who had worked the tunnels and the Guard/Gate House many a time was quite white with worry. Some people refused to continue within the building and asked to leave. That session came to an abrupt end.'

Another set of unusual and possibly paranormal occurrences were related to me by a friend named Matt Newton, who said: 'Around the late 1990s and early 2000s, Fort Amherst started to open their doors to the public for "lock-ins" to experience their paranormal phenomena deep within the tunnels. This came off the back of *Most Haunted*, etc., where people wanted a fright.'

Arnold continues: 'There was a group of about thirty people all of varying ages and a friend of mine wished to experience the paranormal phenomena that Amherst had to offer, having been previously hyped in the local press. We split into our group, after being shown around to get a feel for the place, and were asked to then prepare ourselves for vigils lasting anything from thirty to forty-five minutes, when we would then change positions so that everyone experienced the same area and possible encounter. We were not told of any of the potential inhabitants, for fear of creating hysteria. The network of tunnels beneath Fort Amherst has attracted thousands of ghost hunters over the years. On walking around through the various tunnels, having taken our turn, and having changed to the next location, I saw what could only be described as an explosion of blue sparks, like a mini blue firework display at the base of the stairs, which caught my eye in a split second. I immediately asked my friend if he saw the same display, which he had not, and with this striking image stuck in my mind [I] continued to be excited at the thought of seeing other paranormal events. Upon returning to the central area where we would meet for soup and heat, we were asked if anyone had seen anything. Keen to inform them of my experience, I relayed this to them and was told that what I saw had been a common experience, where some people had seen the image of a Second World War officer standing in full uniform at the bottom of the stairs with a briefcase. Most people that had seen the full manifestation of the officer had started to see blue sparks before he had appeared at the location seen by me.'[6]

---

6. Arnold, Neil, Haunted Chatham (The History Press), p. 28.

Above left: Fort Amherst is one of the most haunted sites in Kent and is also located adjacent to the much-haunted Chatham Dockyard.

Above right: Entrance to the Fort Amherst tunnels.

Right: The network of tunnels beneath Fort Amherst has attracted thousands of ghost hunters over the years.

Above left: Ghost hunter Neil Arnold reported an 'explosion of blue sparks, like a mini blue firework display at the base of the stairs'.

Above right: In this area a witness reported that 'there was a distinct atmosphere of being followed and a feeling of dread, as you would feel if someone was walking close by behind you and was about to charge at you'.

Left: The coffins, which are real, are part of the ghost tour 'fright' experience.

The Plough Inn, Sevenoaks

Eynsford is a delightful ancient village dating back to at least the year 864. The Plough Inn dates to the sixteenth century. It retains little trace of its early origins but is light, airy and serves good food. In keeping with its haunted reputation, it is situated in a quiet strip of road near an ancient bridge with a drive-through ford for larger vehicles. Alan Tigwell, a paranormal investigator, comments on an interesting investigation he undertook into several reports of unusual activity: 'The landlord was interested in finding out more. He explained how there were tales of a ghostly woman who allegedly haunts the outside of the pub and has been seen tapping the window with a coin. Regulars have joked about hearing the tapping when its time for another round! The landlord also told us he believes there is a poltergeist present in the pub, as items are regularly moved when no one is around, or they disappear altogether. While we were filming in the restaurant upstairs, the camcorder was focussed on the lead investigator. A well-known psychic, he was calling out to see if any spirits would make contact. The camcorder I was using was fitted to a tripod and was filming in night shot mode with an additional infrared illuminator to make the picture clearer in the dark room. In the viewfinder I witnessed a dark shape cross the room towards the other investigators. We stopped and viewed the video to try to find out what it was. In the video we could clearly see the shape of a person crossing the room, but at the time, no one was moving and all the investigators were accounted for. We all discussed the potential causes and agreed the most probable answer was that one of the investigators had crossed in front of the infrared illuminator during the recording. This could have cast the shadow into the room which would have then been caught on video. The only problem with this explanation was that everyone said they hadn't been moving at the time. We continued the investigation with no further paranormal events, but by the end of the night the whole team was questioning whether what we caught on camera earlier in the night had a natural explanation. However, when I returned to the Plough Inn several months later for a meal, I discussed the previous event with our waitress who had been absent on the night of the investigation. When I told her about the shadow being recorded, she smiled and explained that she was well aware of the upstairs restaurant being haunted by the figure of a man who crosses the restaurant and descends the stairs. She said that she had witnessed the figure in the room when she was clearing up one night. I realised the lead investigator was standing at the top of the stairs when we had made the recording. Is it possible that we had in fact recorded the ghost rather than the shadow of an investigator?'

Above: A ghostly woman who allegedly haunts the outside of the pub has been seen tapping the window with a coin.

Left: The Plough, Eynsford, interior where a landlord reported there is a poltergeist present in the pub, as items are regularly moved when no one is around, or they disappear altogether.

Eynsford Castle, Sevenoaks

The Eynsford Castle phantom is somewhat contentious. A mysterious monk-like figure, who was not there when a photograph was taken, subsequently appeared in that same photograph.

Jon Wickes took his twelve-year-old son Harry to Eynsford Castle. He took a photograph across the site and believed there was no figure in the shot when he captured the image. The figure was positioned within an opening between a stone wall and the railing of a stairway leading up to the courtyard.

Investigator Alan Tigwell was asked as to whether, in his opinion, the photo showed a ghost. Tigwell commented: 'I went to the site twice last Thursday – in the morning when it first opened, and later on. The purpose of my visit was to ascertain whether there was anything within those walls to explain the picture. I've been investigating the paranormal for over twenty years. The difficulty with looking at things retrospectively

Eynsford Castle ruins – site of a controversial photograph.

Eynsford Castle, similar view.

The controversial monk-like figure can be seen by the footway in the centre. (Photograph Jon Wickes)

is that it's impossible to say exactly what something is. All I can say is that there wasn't anything in the castle itself that could explain that picture. Eynsford Castle is a medieval site and from what Mr Wickes said, there is a legend about a monk being there. In terms of the history of the castle, there was nothing specifically about a monk living there that I could find, but I do believe one of the families who owned it had a son who left to become a monk.'[7]

As a result of the controversy raised by the photograph, Kenny Biddle wrote an investigative article in the September/October 2018 edition of the *Skeptical Inquirer*.[8] Biddle observed that there was no opportunity to verify if the figure was someone else who wandered into the frame. 'The figure is also not "lurking" in the background; it's simply standing there with its back facing the camera.' He continues, 'The father and son pair did not go to the castle looking for ghosts or to investigate the location in a controlled environment. They went there as tourists, nothing more. I am curious as to the other photos he had taken, which may offer a look at any other tourists.'

I quote the relevant points made by Biddle as to the sort of problems facing pictures such as this.

'It's odd that when Wickes finally looked at the image, he reportedly went directly to a paranormal investigator for help (Rowney 2018). Another article states Wickes "looked on the web. That's when I read about a monk being seen in the area" (Joseph 2018) and then contacted the paranormal investigator. In both cases, the figure was associated with a paranormal experience – specifically the ghost of a monk – rather than just another tourist at the castle. That's a big assumption from a photo taken at a location freely open to visitors. … there is a perfectly reasonable explanation: it could be another tourist standing there and Wickes simply didn't notice them. The "ghost" is standing in the courtyard of the ruined castle, and from the distance at which Wickes took the photo, he could have easily missed the relatively small figure in the scene. He could have mistaken the person as being part of the structure or a discoloration of the wall, which is not uncommon when looking through a viewfinder or the small display of the camera. From the image we see that the weather was overcast, leaving the area shaded by clouds and therefore in darker lighting. These lighting conditions dull the details of smaller background objects. When looking at a close-up of the available image, we can see that the figure has a strap going from their left shoulder, down across their back, and ending at their right hip/thigh area. This is most likely a satchel or woman's purse slung over a black coat.'

Biddle says that in a conversation with local researcher Alan Tigwell, he asked about other photos. Tigwell replied, 'I haven't been given any other pictures from Wickes. When I've been involved in cases in the past, I find there does need to be a certain degree of faith in what I'm being told, i.e., taking the person at their word. Wickes was adamant [that] although there were some other people at the castle, none were at this location when he was taking the picture.'

'Although we don't have the other images to look at, we do know that other people were present, and that makes a stray tourist a more plausible explanation than a ghostly monk. The grounds are not very large or extensive, as seen by aerial views

---

7. Tigwell, Alan, *Ghosts in the Garden of England: True Tales of the Paranormal in Kent*.
8. 10/09/2018 – Skeptical Inquirer Volume 42, No. 5 September/October 2018, Kenny Biddle.

from Google Earth. A handful of tourists could easily get into a photograph, especially when the photographer is outside the castle walls.'

I asked Alan what he thought about the figure in the photograph: 'My thoughts on the picture itself? Pretty much the same as any photo with something alleged to be paranormal – its a single snapshot in time; it's impossible to prove one way or another. All you can do is rule out the obvious, which is pretty much what my role in this was: to prove it wasn't anything caused by the structure of the castle, which I did. So, ultimately it all comes down to whether you believe him and his intentions over the photo. Whether its real or fake, there is no way of proving it, but it's a fascinating picture which certainly fires up the imagination!'

Mereworth, Maidstone –
The Forgotten Gate, Park Road

Another interesting account which was shared with Alan Tigwell, which I am repeating, was told by a gentleman called Tom: 'A few years ago I was with my dad and we both saw a ghost. Between Mereworth and Wateringbury, there is a country lane that links two main roads. The country lane goes past St Michael's Church, which is also meant to be haunted, although I've never seen anything there. Along this road, there is a sharp corner which has a huge ornate, but derelict stone gate set back from the road. It's enormous and is on the private property of Mereworth Castle. It's not possible to go through it – there is no path or lane and it's all fenced off and overgrown. Mereworth Castle is very old and goes back hundreds of years. I think the current house was built in around 1700 and is a listed building. Unfortunately, you can't go into the castle as it's privately owned. The country lane leads around the gate and has quite a wide corner where you can park. My dad used to park here

55302. Mereworth Castle from the North.

Mereworth Castle from an old postcard, c. 1905. A father and son reported that 'a horse came galloping out of the gate with a man riding it directly towards where we were standing'.

and walk our dog in the fields. I would sometimes go with him and it was on one of our walks that we saw something supernatural. We had parked up in the space at the corner and were getting out of the car when we heard what sounded like a whip crack. It's not often you hear something like that, so we weren't sure what it was. We looked around and couldn't see anything – there were no other cars or people around and by now everything was quiet (it's quite an isolated location in the country). We carried on and got the dog out the back of the car and went for our walk. About an hour later, we had just got back to where the car was parked and we heard another loud crack, but this time it was followed by the sounds of horse hooves. It sounded like it was coming from over in the direction of the old gate, so we looked over to see what it was. I didn't think any horse could possibly be galloping that fast based on the sounds I was hearing, especially as the area around the gate is wooded and so overgrown. My dad and I were asking each other what we thought it could be, when a horse came galloping out of the gate with a man riding it directly towards where we were standing. What made this a totally bizarre experience was that the horse and man, although appearing solid, were racing through all the foliage and they also came directly through, not over, the fence. As they came across the road, the sounds of the hooves didn't change either; they sounded as though they were still on packed earth rather than the road surface. My dad grabbed me by my collar and pulled me away from the car just as the man and the horse went through it, making the car rock slightly. They then went through the hedge and trees behind us and disappeared, the sounds of the hooves stopping abruptly. My dad and I went back into the field but we couldn't see them anywhere. We were both a little shaken but to ease the tension, my dad said, "That must have been the ghostly highwayman." It turns out in West Peckham, a short distance away, there are stories about a highwayman called Jack Diamond who haunts a house which he apparently used to live in. I've always assumed ghosts of highwaymen would wear the stereotypical garb you see on the telly, with the hat and the long black coat, but our phantom highwayman didn't wear any of that. He was in a brown leather coat and a pair of loose black trousers with brown boots. No hat was worn, but on the horse were a couple of saddlebags and a whip poking out. Thinking about it, none of the clothes he wore were like what you'd expect a horse rider to wear today; they seemed to be in keeping with something you'd expect to see in the age of highwaymen.' The stories about Jack Diamond say his ghost appears on Friday the 13th at the West Peckham house, but this was a Saturday in late July, so maybe this could be the location he haunts the rest of the year?[9]

---

9. Tigwell, Alan, *Ghosts in the Garden of England: True Tales of the Paranormal in Kent*.

Sandling Road, Maidstone

The so-called 'Bat Beast of Kent' has something for almost everyone, including an unidentified flying creature and a UFO. The incident has captured the online popular imagination. Brent Swancer, in an article headed 'The Mysterious Bat Beast of Kent', 6 September 2021,[10] has probably one of the best descriptions of the 'Bat Beast'.

'Of all of the weird cases of strange entities, some of the oddest are of flying humanoids, and some of these can be pretty bizarre indeed. The setting for this particular weird tale is the historic Sandling Park in Maidstone, Kent, a quaint woodland established upon the ancient wood of Westenhanger. It is a peaceful, quiet place with placid meadows, ornamental woodland gardens, and vast expanses of rhododendrons, and by all appearances does not seem to be the sort of place where one would expect to encounter mysterious monsters, but on one cold November night in 1963 this would change. On this evening, friends John Flaxton and Mervyn Hutchinson and two other teen boys were walking home through the park on a road that meanders through. They were coming from a party, and all of them were in good spirits, chatting away and laughing, when something unusual caught their attention in the sky, and from here there would be a rather strange series of events with an entity that has never been fully explained away. When they looked up, they saw a very brightly lit "golden oval-shaped" object measuring a few meters in diameter that seemed to be hovering over a nearby field. Whatever it was, it was described as intensely bright, much brighter than any star or planet in the sky, and more brilliant that any aircraft. The object then began to approach them, and they began to run as it followed, after which the object moved back to its original position. As the boys looked on in astonishment, the object then suddenly began to drop down, sinking below the treeline out of sight. At first they thought it was perhaps a helicopter, but the object had been completely, eerily silent, and so they were driven by curiosity to walk off towards the field to see what it was. Things would get even stranger from there. They soon made it to where the object had come down, but were surprised to see no sign of it. There was no more light, no orb, no trace that anything had ever been there at all. It was all quite baffling, as all of them had seen it, so they knew they had not been imagining things. As they looked around in puzzlement they could then hear the rustling of bushes nearby, and a strange chill suddenly materialised, as well as a charge in the air like static electricity. When they looked to see what was making the noise, a figure like something out of a nightmare emerged from the gloom. There, shambling out into the moonlight, was a dark, hairy figure standing roughly 5 feet tall and with large, webbed feet like those of a duck. The torso had no arms, but rather

10. https://mysteriousuniverse.org/2021/09/the-mysterious-bat-beast-of-kent/

two large and prominent bat-like wings, and most bizarrely of all was that it had no discernible head. This monstrosity then sort of waddled towards them like a penguin, before suddenly spreading its wings and launching itself through the air at them. The boys screamed and bolted away as fast as they could, and the creature passed right over them to veer off and disappear into the night. The witnesses went to the nearest police station to breathlessly tell of their surreal and terrifying experience, but of course no one believed them. They were told to stop telling tall tales and go home, thinking that at best they had been merely freaked out by a large owl, but it would soon turn out that there was perhaps something more to this. Less than a week later, a local man by the name of Keith Croucher, who had no connection to any of the boys, claimed to have seen a brightly glowing object on the same evening as their sightings, and just two days after this there would be another report from a man named John McGoldrick. He claimed that he had gone out with a friend to investigate after having learned of these sightings, and that they had soon found several large, webbed footprints measuring 24 inches long and 9 inches across, as well as an area of brush that seemed to have been flattened by something large and heavy passing through. He also claimed that they had seen a strange glow coming through the trees at one point, although they didn't see the creature itself. After this, several other reports would come in from people in the area of the park claiming to have seen strange lights in the sky and a winged creature flying about near the area. The sightings of the 'Bat Beast of Kent' were soon making heavy rounds in the newspapers, and they would also appear in *The Flying Saucer Review*, as well as get a mention in John Keel's *The Mothman Prophecies*. The case was unique in that it seemed to blend elements of ufology, cryptozoology, and the paranormal, being very hard to categorize as any one of these. To ufologists this was clearly a case of a UFO and its alien occupant, whereas cryptozoologists thought it was some unidentified avian monster and ghost hunters thought it was a ghost, spirit, or demon.'

Maidstone Road Cemetery, Matfield

Alan Tigwell very kindly gave me permission to reproduce the following ghostly encounter. I visited the cemetery in the spring of 2021 curious to retrace the steps of Stephen T., whom Alan had interviewed. I did note that through the gate approximately where Stephen T. said he saw the apparitions, there was the grave of a young child. I looked at all the angles and followed the steps described by Stephen. The cemetery is clearly visible from the road as is the area he described. I found his description quite plausible.

'This happened a few years ago near to where I live, when I was driving towards the village of Matfield from the direction of the A21. Just as you enter the village, on the right there is an old, small cemetery where some (but not all) of the graves have been moved because of the building of houses. I believe they were moved up to the church on the outskirts of the village, but I may be wrong on that. It was mid-afternoon on a summer's day. As I was coming up to the cemetery, I glanced over and saw a man and a child planting flowers on a grave just by the fence and gate, nearest the road. I could clearly see the people – the man was wearing a dark grey suit and his hair was slicked back. I remember thinking how it was the same style my grandad used to have when he was younger. The little girl was facing the road and was wearing an old-style dress with a hat; I could see her blonde curls coming out from under it. As I passed, I slowed down to look at the man planting the flowers; I could see him using a gardening tool to dig some of the earth away. My gaze then fell onto the girl, who was looking directly at me, who then raised her arms up and held them out like children do when they want to be picked up. I'll never forget the look on her face; she had a look of pure loneliness and longing. My gaze went back to the road. I couldn't shake the feeling of how completely out of place they looked, and I have to admit, I was distressed at the look the girl had given me. Looking at the cemetery, which is around 100 yards up the road, I couldn't see either the man or the girl. As I arrived at the cemetery gate a few short moments later, my suspicions were confirmed and they were gone. They certainly couldn't have walked out of the cemetery and up the road as I'd be able to see them (it's a long straight road), so I assumed they must have gone to the back of the cemetery, which is behind a large tree. I looked at the grave where the man had been digging a spot for the flowers he was holding, but the grass which covered the entire cemetery was undisturbed and there were no flowers either. I opened the metal gate, which made a loud squeaking sound as it moved, and stepped into the cemetery. Even though it was a nice, warm summer's afternoon, it was like I had stepped into a chiller cabinet. I was shocked at the sudden change in temperature, so I hurried towards the back and made my way around the tree, calling out "hello?"

I looked at the grave where the man had been digging a spot for the flowers he was holding, but the grass which covered the entire cemetery was undisturbed and there were no flowers either.

as I went. There was no one there and also no way for anyone to leave the cemetery without me seeing (like I say, it is very small, only around 100 yards in length and 10 in width). By this point, I was spooked, so I hurried back to my car and left the coldness behind. I've since learned that the pub I stopped my car at is also meant to be haunted. After that experience, each time I drive through the village and past the old cemetery, I never look over into it anymore. I always get the feeling I'll see the girl and the man again!'[11]

11. Tigwell, Alan, *Ghosts in the Garden of England: True Tales of the Paranormal in Kent.*

View of cemetery gate from direction described towards the pub diagonally opposite.

Pembury, near Tunbridge Wells

Anne West lived at Old Bayhall Manor and died in the 1830s aged thirty-seven years. She had a fear that she might be buried alive. She believed that although she might appear to be dead, she could in fact be in a coma or suspended animation and would wake to find herself underground. She inserted a clause in her will, that after her death her body should be placed in an open tomb or small individual vault, above ground in the churchyard of Pembury Old Church, a mile or so from her home. The vault was to be covered with a 'box' or 'table-tomb', four-sided with a heavy flat top and at one end, the east side, a grille was to be inserted and so constructed that it could be opened from inside the vault. The coffin, resting on a low support, was to have its lid left unscrewed and over the face of the body a small window was to be inserted in the coffin lid. Furthermore, Anne West's bailiff was to be instructed to bring to the vault each evening just before sunset a basket of food and a flask of wine, to be placed near the grille where she would be able to reach them and also summon help from any passer-by. This practice was to be continued for one year after her burial.

These instructions were duly carried out to the letter — for around a month after Anne West was buried and then, suddenly and mysteriously, the bailiff disappeared. The churchyard is or was reputedly haunted by the ghost of Anne West and her bailiff. The ghostly figure of the bailiff is said to appear along the cart track and carriage road from Old Bayhall Manor, until where it reaches the village main road.

Paranormal researcher Frederick Sanders described Old Bayhall, when some structure still remained, as a derelict manor. 'At night' he writes, 'this ruinous edifice presents itself as an "eerie pile"; it lies in a valley, surrounded by wooded hills … The ruined manor is alive with the scurrying and squeaking of rats while the monotonous sound of water dripping into one of the old, blocked-up cellars adds to the eeriness of the place. From time to time sounds of movement that might be thought to be human beings are caused by rabbits in the long grass or moving over the broken surfaces of stones and rubble in the vicinity of this once-haunted place …'

Sanders and a friend decided to spend a night there. As nothing happened they made their way to Pembury Old Church and stationed themselves inside the churchyard from soon after eleven o'clock, staying there until around half an hour after midnight. Paranormal author Peter Underwood related that 'they illuminated the interior of Anne West's open vault by directing the beam of a torch downwards through the small grille and they could make out the crumbled remnants of the coffin and the remains of Anne West herself. Her skull lay upon the floor of the tomb, minus the lower jaw'. At half an hour to midnight, Sanders placed his self-illuminating watch on the flat top of the tomb just above the position of the grille. 'A sudden drop in temperature of psychic origin might quite possibly stop the watch, as sudden extremes of cold are apt to affect the delicate mechanisms of watches and clocks', he pointed out. 'Also, if there happened to be any poltergeistic influence around, the watch might get moved, dropped or flung about.' As Sanders 'stood silently near the old tomb a noise like a subdued rustling became audible, followed by a light thump, followed again by a jerking, gritty sound'. They glimpsed a small black form bounding along the pathway. It was a black cat at full gallop and it quickly disappeared into the gloom on the further side of the graveyard. They then 'gradually became aware of a light, almost phosphorescent, glow suffusing the south side of the church at short irregular intervals'. This, they discovered, was caused by the light from the moon high up in the night sky. Then 'just before 11.40 p.m.' Sanders writes, 'my co-watcher went over to the church porch and went inside to get out of the cold, damp and windy atmosphere; he did not seem at all hopeful about seeing anything. Meanwhile I moved nearer the tomb where I could hear my watch ticking, very faintly, and I then stationed myself in the centre of the church path where I was almost within touching distance of the watch. At approximately 11.40 p.m. I felt three taps upon my right shoulder; it felt just as though someone behind me had touched me with their finger ends or the tip of a light stick, as if to say: stand aside please. I turned at once: there was no one there. I turned my face to the sky and wind: no drops of rain were falling. I could see nothing

Anne West's open vault tomb. 'I then stationed myself in the centre of the church path .... I felt three taps upon my right shoulder.'

on my shoulder and I was wearing a light-coloured raincoat at the time. There were no bushes or trees with overhanging branches from which droplets of accumulated moisture could have fallen anywhere near me. Kenneth Jefferey came quickly from the church porch at my call. I asked him to shine his torch on my right shoulder to look for a mark or any sign of moisture. He did so and found nothing. Then to make sure, I divested myself of the raincoat and made a scrupulous examination. I could find no clue to the three taps. Ten minutes later I placed the watch as near as I could to the grille and both of us stood on the grass at the end of the tomb and kept our eyes fixed on the watch. For ten minutes nothing happened. I replaced the watch in my coat pocket and shortly afterwards we left the area. I moved nearer the tomb where I could hear my watch ticking, very faintly, and I then stationed myself in the centre of the church path where I felt three taps upon my right shoulder; it felt just as though someone behind me had touched me.'[12]

Exterior of St Peter's Church, Pembury.

12. Underwood, Peter, *Ghosts of Kent: Illustrated Edition.*

'From (the former) Old Bayhall Manor, along the lonely cart track and carriage road until it reaches the village main road, the ghostly figure of the bailiff is said to walk.'

Bayham Abbey, Tunbridge Wells

Bayham Abbey is an English Heritage site. At the time of writing in 2022 entry is free. Despite it being a bright sunny day on my visit to the abbey, there was an atmosphere of sadness amidst the desolation that remains. The site is believed to be haunted 'on still, moonless nights', by 'a line of monks'. Plainchant has also been heard and the smell of incense detected by tourists at the site. I felt that a real sadness lay in the area of the graves of the two infant children of the Marquis and Marchioness of Camden who died in 1868 and 1869.

Poignant memorial to the children of the Marquis and Marchioness of Camden who died in their infancy and are buried nearby.

The graves of the two infant children of the Marquis and Marchioness of Camden add to the sad, brooding air of the ancient ruins.

A procession of phantom monks are said to haunt the ruins.

Old Soar Manor, Sevenoaks

Of all the sites I visited when writing this book, Old Soar Manor was probably the most haunting and atmospheric. Despite being a National Trust site, it is quiet and remote, and sits in a lane surrounded by fields. On the day I visited there were no other visitors. The building felt dark and gloomy. The story goes that an eighteenth-century dairy maid called Jenny accidentally drowned herself whilst she was pregnant. She was descried as 'quite pleasant, but quiet and shy', and was regarded locally as being a simpleton. She fell in love with a farmworker called Ted, who was ten years older than her. He took advantage of her feelings towards him but was not so serious himself. At Christmas 1775, Jenny was employed to assist in the preparation of the food for the Geary family Christmas dinner. It was during the celebrations that the family priest, drunk with ale, stumbled into Jenny in the kitchen as she was trying to do her work. He dragged her into the barn where he seduced her, she being far too scared to protest, for he was one of the gentry. Jenny became pregnant. Midsummer came and Jenny had been totally disowned by her father and Ted refused to have anything to do with her. She had nobody to turn to. She could not go to 'the master', because he would not have believed her and she would have been dismissed. There was only one thing she could do, and that was to visit the child's father.

The following Sunday afternoon, Jenny visited the chapel where she knew the priest would be. She heard the priest playing the small organ and she entered and crossed the floor to the corner of the room. The priest stopped playing and walked over to the piscina (a basin in which the priest ritually washes his hands). One look at the girl made him realize the reason for her visit. He was in a dilemma. Being a Roman Catholic priest, he could not marry the girl, even if he had wanted to, and at the same time, if it was to become known that he was the father of the child, he would be defrocked. When he learned that Ted no longer wanted to have anything to do with her, he advised her that she should find another boyfriend and marry him for the sake of the child. After dispensing that bit of hypocritical advice he left the chapel. Jenny felt faint with hunger, for she had not eaten a morsel for days because of all her worries. The room began to spin and she rose giddily and went over to the piscina, thinking that a little water would help her. She fainted, and in doing so struck her head on the side of the bowl. When the priest returned, he found her dead – having knocked herself unconscious she had drowned, ironically, in 2 inches of 'holy water'. It was assumed that Jenny had committed suicide, although it would have been difficult for her to have killed herself in such a manner. She was buried in unconsecrated ground.

The story continues. In the 1970s there were reports of lights being seen in the empty building, which by this time was in the hands of the National Trust. Music was also heard coming from the empty chapel. People reported the sudden dropping of temperature in the chapel and the feeling of a ghostly presence. It was in 1972 that

Above: The building was constructed in around 1290.

Left: It was in 1972 that a long grey cloak was seen hanging in the chapel, but it disappeared in front of the witness's eyes.

The Paranormal Database reports that 'lights flicker around the chapel after dark'.

In 1972 the phantom figure of a priest was seen bending over the piscina.

a long grey cloak was seen hanging in the chapel but this disappeared in front of the witness' eyes. A few days later the phantom figure of a priest was seen bending over the piscina. It around this same time that an old man said he had been employed on the farm in the early twentieth century, when the building was being used as a store for valuable straw and hay, that he had often slept the night on the ground floor, to guard the hay from thieves. He frequently heard a woman's footsteps pacing the floor of the empty room upstairs. The room was the chapel, and the footsteps were only heard in the month of June.[13]

13. Source: Ghosts of the Southeast, a website describing haunted houses in Southeastern England.

Pluckley, Ashford

Pluckley appeared in the Guinness Book of Records as the most haunted village in England with twelve 'official' ghosts. On the day I visited Pluckley none of the supernatural inhabitants appeared, although I followed the standard ghost hunter's trail! The village claims a highwayman who hides in a tree at the Pinnock, a phantom coach and horses seen around the village.

Other reported spirits are the ghost of a gypsy woman who drowned in a stream at the Pinnock, a miller seen at Mill Hill, the hanging body of a schoolmaster in Dicky Buss's Lane, a colonel who hanged himself in Park Wood, a man smothered by a wall

A phantom coach and horses has allegedly been seen around the village.

of clay who drowned at the brickworks, and the 'Lady of Rose Court', who is said to have poisoned herself in despair over a love triangle.

St Nicholas' Church has a supernatural concentration. Located at the top of the first aisle in the church is the Dering Chapel, where numerous members of the family lie buried. The Red Lady, reputedly a member of the Dering family, haunts the churchyard. A small white dog has also been reported in the same location. There is a 'White Lady', apparently buried inside seven coffins and an oak sarcophagus, who also haunts the church in the same location, seen in the upper section of the window to your right. The sighting is often accompanied by the sound of knocking coming from the family vault beneath your feet.

In the early 1970s, in the hope of recording supernatural phenomena, a group of psychic researchers persuaded the then rector, the Revd John Pittock, to allow them to spend a night locked inside the church. Armed with their cameras, tape recorders, thermometers and other apparatus, they settled down to watch and wait. When the vicar came to let them out the next morning they complained of having spent an uneventful night, the boredom of which had been alleviated only by the vicar's dog, who had come to visit them from time to time. 'Actually,' the vicar commented, 'I don't have a dog.'

St Nicholas' Church, Pluckley.

The Red Lady, reputedly a member of the Dering family, haunts the churchyard of St Nicholas' Church. A small white dog has also been reported.

A strange, dancing light has frequently been seen in the upper section of the window to your right. It is often accompanied by the sound of knocking coming from the Dering family vault.

No section on Pluckley would be complete without mention of the Screaming Woods, otherwise known as the Dering Woods, between the villages of Smarden and Pluckley. One online site reports that they are reputed to be 'the most haunted woods in Britain and they were given their name because of the many reports of people hearing terrifying screams coming from the forest at night or footsteps and whispers during days of fog'. There is no evidence that the sounds are anything but natural.

Left: A Ghostbusters sign at the entrance to the Dering Woods, otherwise known as the 'Screaming Woods'.

Below: The Screaming Woods are part of the Pluckley ghost legend.

The Black Horse Pub, Pluckley

The day I visited The Black Horse it was permanently closed – probably due to lockdown – but I'm happy to report that it has now reopened. The Black Horse lies in the middle of the village and has a history of reported incidents. The building dates back to the 1470s when it was a farmhouse belonging to the Dering family. It has featured on several paranormal television programmes. One of the ghosts regularly moves the glasses and possessions of the staff and customers and the ghost of a child has been seen in the pub.

The author of London-walking-tours comments that the manager of the pub in 1997 told him that on her first Sunday at work she was enjoying a cup of tea just prior to opening for the busy Sunday lunchtime session. She noticed a glass on the shelf

The Black Horse pub dates from the fifteenth century and has operated as a pub for around 300 years.

Allegedly one of the ghosts regularly moves the glasses and possessions of the staff and customers.

above the bar move just a little. As she watched it, she was astonished when it began to slide along the length of the shelf, stopping when it reached the edge. Other ghostly activities included an unseen hand that lifted cutlery from the dresser and arranged it neatly on the side; a spot in the kitchen where the pet dogs would stop abruptly and bark at something, or someone, that only they could see; and an upstairs room that the dogs refused to enter.[14]

Paranormal investigator Alan Tigwell visited The Black Horse on a Halloween evening, but had no success ghost hunting. He says, 'We had arrived and parked in the gravel car park behind the pub. Even though it was October and was quite cold outside, the car full of people had soon become too warm, so we all had our windows open. We were all sat in the car, talking about the night's events (or lack of them), when one of my friends asked, "do you hear that?" We all became deathly silent and listened. Initially nothing happened, but then we heard footsteps on the gravel outside the car. They became quite loud, as if someone was walking towards us, but there was no one there. The sound of the footsteps crunching on the gravel stopped outside the passenger door for a moment, then started walking around the car, round and round. We all looked out of our windows, not quite believing it was what we thought it was. I could see indentations in the gravel where someone had walked, when a friend shouted, "look at the window!" We all turned our attention to the windscreen to see a small handprint appear and the sound of a little girl giggle. We all jumped out of the car and looked all around but couldn't find anyone. I've been back to the pub and car park several times to see if the girl would revisit, but never had anything else happen.'[15]

---

14. https://www.london-walking-tours.co.uk/free-tours/haunted-pluckley.htm
15. Tigwell, Alan. Ghosts in the Garden of England: True tales of the paranormal in Kent.

St Mary's Church Ruins nr Pluckley, Little Chart

I came across these ruins almost by accident on my journey into Pluckley, which is a short distance further down the road. I pulled over into a layby. I felt that even if the ruins had no recorded paranormal events, it felt as if they should have, with their dark, gloomy and overgrown presence – untended graves scattered the site. The tower was built by Sir John Darell. The church was hit by a flying bomb during the Second World and was virtually demolished.

The only recorded event I could find for the ruins came from an encounter reported by Alan Tigwell, which he kindly gave me permission to quote in full. 'Steve and I are really into all things spooky and scary. We've been on lots of ghost walks, stayed in haunted hotels and even paid to go on paranormal investigations with an events company. Unfortunately, we've never seen a ghost. That was until October last year. For people in Kent who are interested in this sort of stuff, Pluckley is the pinnacle of places to go and visit. It has a huge reputation of being haunted and has been featured in the Guinness Book of World Records as being the most haunted village in Kent. Based on this, we decided to spend the day visiting the different haunted sites. We found that a lot of them were in privately owned homes, so all we could do was take a quick glance and not linger about as it would look too suspicious! There was also a story about a haunted pub but that wasn't there anymore – it had been converted into houses. Apart from those, we had a great time; we even bumped into a group of other people who were doing the exact same thing as us! Unfortunately, we didn't see anything remotely paranormal. We had a quick bite to eat in The Black Horse pub (another haunted location) and then headed out of Pluckley. The group we had spoken to earlier in the day had told us about another place that would be good to visit. It was a ruined church in Little Chart, not too far away, and luckily for us, was on our way home. We found the church and stepped over what used to be the wall. There were a few houses behind the church which we hadn't seen when we parked, so we tried to make sure anyone looking out of the windows wouldn't spot us. It's not like we were up to no good; we just didn't want the police to be called, which apparently happens to would-be ghost hunters in Pluckley. It seemed small for a church; we could see where the altar would have been, although nothing remained. The main architecture which was left standing was the tower area and the open archway of the door to the church. Just to the left of this was a boarded-up door which we assumed would lead to the upper level of the tower. We could see the open door upstairs which should anyone come running through, they would just fall down to the ground floor again – a fall which would probably kill the person. It's no wonder it was boarded up. We tried to see if we could prise the wood boards off so we could go look upstairs, but it was solid and there was no movement at all. Whoever built this was a very good carpenter! One of the pieces of information the group from earlier made us aware of was that the altar was built facing the wrong way. Apparently, they are meant to face a certain direction and this one didn't follow the correct template or pattern. For this reason, it is believed the church ruins are a prime location for something paranormal to happen. I don't know whether this is true, but the people from earlier were certainly convincing! We had a longer look around the back of the church and saw many overgrown but ornate graves. On our way back to the car, we decided to go take a look at the tower again. We walked over to where the boarded-up door was, and almost immediately we both heard a scratching coming from behind it. It wasn't particularly loud to start with, but enough for us to hear. The scratching continued on the inside of the door, mixed with a few light knocks. Between the makeshift door and the wall there was a very thin crack which we could look through. Steve peeked in but couldn't see anything because it was so dark. I gave him my phone, which had a light on it, and he tried again. This time, he took a look and turned to me and explained he could see the stone steps leading to the upstairs part of the church; he said they were covered in dust or sawdust or some other substance. He looked back into the crack to see what else could be seen. As I was about to ask whether he could see what was making the noise, he gasped and looked at me with a huge grin on his face. He exclaimed, "I just saw a ghost! It's going up the stairs." We took a few steps back, so we could see the upper part of the tower and Steve pointed and said "Look!" Out of the open door at the top, we saw a white figure-like shape come gliding out. I expected it to fall to the

The haunted ruined church in Little Chart near Pluckley.

'Out of the open door at the top, we saw a white figure-like shape come gliding out. I expected it to fall to the ground, but it didn't. It just glided out into the open above where we were standing and disappeared into the air.'

ground, but it didn't. It just glided out into the open above where we were standing and disappeared into the air. Steve explained to me when he had looked back through the gap and had shone the light into the space, he had seen a man looking back at him. However, the man wasn't a solid person; his features weren't clear and seemed to be translucent. Steve said that the ghost had turned around and glided up the stairs. He went on to explain that he used the term glided because he couldn't see the legs moving – the lower part of the figure was "wispy and smoke like", if that makes sense at all. We've since suggested it looked a bit like a male version of the library ghost in *Ghostbusters*, without the horrible creature it turns into of course! We waited around for a while to see if it came back, trying to look behind the boarded-up door many times, but nothing else appeared for us and there was no scratching heard either. We did note that whatever the dust was on the stairs, it hadn't been disturbed at all by the ghost travelling up the stairs. After a while we headed back to the car, took a final look at the tower just in case the ghost was there again (it wasn't of course!) and headed home. All in all, it was a fantastic day, rounded off with us seeing our very first ghost!'[16]

---

16. Tigwell, Alan, *Ghosts in the Garden of England: True Tales of the Paranormal in Kent*.

Rochester Cathedral

Rochester Cathedral is situated opposite the castle. Charles Dickens' ghost allegedly haunts the graveyard and is often seen pausing to read inscriptions on some of the graves. He is also said to wander the castle moat as well. Another spirit wearing a blue blazer has been observed walking the length of the nave before disappearing into the wall where an old archway, now bricked up, led to the old churchyard.

A ghostly organ has been heard, as well as footsteps in a kitchen used by the verger and staff at the end of a dimly lit passageway. In 2008, as the cathedral was shutting a figure standing at the end of the row near the main entrance door was photographed. The figure, although blurred, appears to be clergyman in dark garments, clutching his hands by his chest and captured, mid stride, around 100 yards away. The photographer claims there was nobody there. Author and investigator Neil Arnold comments that 'recently, a ghostly monk has also been observed in the crypt. During the early 1990s an organist scholar had ventured into the cathedral of a night to practice when he heard the sound of the organ, suggesting someone had got into the cathedral and had been playing it. However, when the man ventured towards the organ the sounds suddenly stopped, spooking the organist. He fled from the building.'[17]

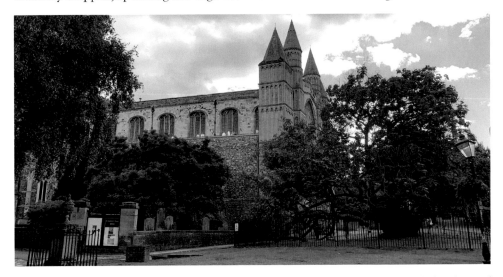

Rochester Cathedral. A ghostly monk has also been observed in the crypt and the ghost of Charles Dickens in the graveyard.

17. Arnold, Neil, *Haunted Rochester* (The History Press), p. 59.

Rochester Castle

The castle is an impressive, brooding, ancient ruin which houses a number of spectres. The most famous is the 'White Lady', believed to be the spectre of Lady Blanche de Warenne who was killed by an arrow which struck her in her breast during a siege in 1264. Her ghost is allegedly sighted with an arrow protruding from her chest. Author Peter Underwood, during the 1980s, mentioned an investigator friend called Mr Sanders who 'one night, whilst accompanied by the castle caretaker, two photographers and a police sergeant, heard footsteps on one of the stone spiral staircases of the North East Tower. A man's voice was also heard echoing through the corridors. On another visit, Mr Sanders, accompanied by his wife, and those already mentioned, claimed to have heard two sets of footsteps in the tower.'

One of the spirits said to roam amongst the graves is that of a white lady searching for her child. Neil Arnold refers to a large-scale paranormal investigation that took place during the early 1990s: 'Eighteen investigators, split into six groups, entered the castle on 4 July 1992. A reporter from the *Observer* newspaper accompanied the investigation. They witnessed the switching on and off of the security light in the keep (even though no presence triggered the sensor). Strange metallic clicks and heavy thumps were heard in the same location, and on one occasion footsteps were heard during the early hours, also from the keep. Staff working at the castle over the years have also recorded several strange incidents.'

One report stated that in September 2005: 'I visited Rochester Castle in the evening of a September day, and was looking up at the round tower when I saw a glint of something. To my amazement as I focused I saw what seemed to be a man in armour and he seemed to be pointing his bow and arrow towards the ground. He then vanished. It left me very shaken.' November 2005: 'When visiting the castle, I was walking near the top with my wife, and we heard footsteps. To our horror we looked across to the flag tower and saw a man dressed in brown, with bow and quiver of arrows. As soon as we saw him he disappeared.' March 2006: 'My husband and I were walking through the castle (our third visit) when we realised there were footsteps behind us. We just thought it was other visitors, but my husband looked up and saw what seemed to be a lady dressed in a long, white dress walking in the opposite direction along one of the walkways. I caught sight of her as she disappeared into a doorway. It shocked us both at the time, but she did seem very peaceful.' December 2007: Report of a visitor seeing a lady in medieval garments, walking down the spiral stone staircase of the castle. The woman walked through a wall and vanished. 2010: 'Want to report my experience in the gallery. I was standing, looking over into the pit and felt as if I was being watched, then out of nowhere, I heard a woman whisper into my ear.' 2010: 'Have just seen a transparent figure in one of the upper floors of the castle. It walked through an archway and along as though there were still a floor in place. I couldn't believe my eyes.'

The mysterious lady in white may be the most known ghost of the castle, but other figures and activity are reported too. A fact sheet given out by the castle staff states: 'In the chapel, which now has the model of the castle in it, and directly above the shop, which would originally have been the fore building, there is a presence of a man, possibly a man of the cloth (priest).' From time to time he will appear to staff and visitors, walking around the room with his head bowed or even looking at them waiting for them to speak to him. Occasionally a visitor will ask if there is a ghost in the chapel, because they had a feeling of being watched as they walked around the room. When you are in the shop and the keep is empty and quiet you can hear him walking around slowly in the chapel. Sometimes the footsteps are much louder and heavier. As yet those working here have not discovered if it is the same ghost or one yet to make themselves known. Some members of staff and general visitors have heard noises and experienced odd feelings as they walk around the castle. Whilst walking around the gallery some have heard footsteps both quick and slow, as if someone is walking and running. The sound of skirts rustling and brushing the ground has also been heard. Going around the gallery, as you near the round tower, some have said that they have heard a woman sobbing. On the battlements – which some people found scary due to how high up you were – there was a time when a couple of visitors suddenly felt gripped by a terrible fear of being found.

In February 2008 a tall, darkly clad figure was observed by a witness who became extremely distressed after the sighting. During the same year a witness reported, 'I have just been to the castle and got the fright of my life. I heard footsteps behind me and looked round and in the shadows I saw a hooded figure that said, in no uncertain terms, "Get out!" Strangely, this report echoed a similar account earlier in the year when a couple visiting the castle wrote in the book, 'My husband and I were walking around the middle section of the castle when, without warning, it went icy cold all around us and we both heard a voice, in a whispery tone, say, "Go away!" In 2009 a couple also noted a sudden drop in temperature and a voice rasping, "Go away!' In the same year another witness reported seeing a monk walking in the area of the chapel. Another couple in the room had not seen the hooded figure. In 2010, Kevin Payne, who was visiting the castle with his sister Claire, was randomly taking photographs inside the castle. Claire took a few shots also. When the photographs were developed they were both shocked to see a monk in a black habit. Although only the arm and shoulder of the habit are visible in the photo, they claim there was no one else in the room when the photo was taken! Investigations into the monks in and around the castle have proven that they were in fact of the Benedictine order and wore a black habit. Other paranormal activity in the castle appears less dramatic than the 'white lady' or hooded figure. In January 2006 a married couple visiting the castle were alarmed by a sudden white fog which appeared near the ladder of the gloomy cesspit. In October 2006 a man with white hair was seen gazing out of one of the windows. The following year, in January, a lady reported to the castle staff that she'd been tapped on the shoulder by an unseen presence, and in the June of 2007 a man reported he'd seen a strange mist and two orb-like objects emerging from the 'well'. During the autumn it was reported that a bright, illuminating light had been seen in the gallery.[18]

18. Arnold, Neil, *Haunted Rochester* (The History Press).

Rochester Castle has many phantoms, but the 'white lady', believed to be the spectre of Lady Blanche de Warenne, who was killed during a siege in 1264, is the best known.

The Cooper's Arms, Rochester

Several inns in Rochester are said to be haunted. The Cooper's Arms, probably the oldest public house in Kent, has the ghost of a grey-robed monk-like figure that emerges through the wall of the bar and after disappearing leaves behind a cold and clammy atmosphere. Eight hundred years ago the building formed part of an old priory. The ghost is thought to be that of one of the brethren who was walled-up alive for some forgotten sin. This ghost is said to manifest most frequently during the month of November,[19] sliding pints along the counter, resulting in them crashing to the floor. The monk has also been sighted near the cellar. There is said to be another rarely mentioned ghost at the pub, the spirit of an old man with wild, staring eyes.

Probably the oldest pub in Kent, the ghost is thought to be that of a murdered monk who had been walled-up alive.

---

19. Underwood, Peter, *Ghosts of Kent: Illustrated Edition* Kindle edition, pp. 163–164.

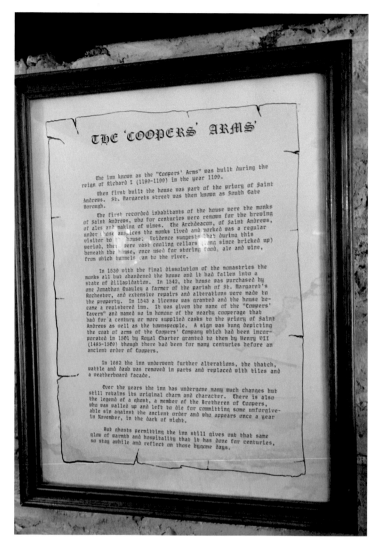

The inn known as the "Coopers' Arms" was built during the reign of Richard I (1189-1199) in the year 1199.

When first built the house was part of the priory of Saint Andrews. St. Margarets street was then known as South Gate Borough.

The first recorded inhabitants of the house were the monks of Saint Andrews, who for centuries were renown for the brewing of ales and making of wines. The Archdeacon, of Saint Andrews, under those auspices the monks lived and worked was a regular visitor to the house. Evidence suggests that during this period, there were vast cooling cellars (long since bricked up) beneath the house, once used for storing food, ale and wine, from which tunnels ran to the river.

In 1539 with the final dissolution of the monasteries the monks all but abandoned the house and it had fallen into a state of dillapidation. In 1542, the house was purchased by one Jonathan Quayley a farmer of the parish of St. Margaret's Rochester, and extensive repairs and alterations were made to the property. In 1543 a license was granted and the house became a registered inn. It was given the name of the "Coopers' tavern" and named so in honour of the nearby cooperage that had for a century or more supplied casks to the priory of Saint Andrews as well as the townspeople. A sign was hung depicting the coat of arms of the Coopers' Company which had been incorporated in 1501 by Royal Charter granted to them by Henry VII (1485-1509) though there had been for many centuries before an ancient order of Coopers.

In 1682 the inn underwent further alterations, the thatch, wattle and daub was removed in parts and replaced with tiles and a weatherboard facade.

Over the years the inn has undergone many such changes but still retains its original charm and character. There is also the legend of a ghost, a member of the Bretheren of Coopers, who was walled up and left to die for committing some unforgiveable sin against the ancient order and who appears once a year in November, in the dark of night.

But ghosts permitting the inn still gives out that same glow of warmth and hospitality that it has done for centuries, so stay awhile and reflect on those bygone days.

The Coopers Arms. The Coopers Arms, situated on St Margaret's Street at No. 10, is one of the oldest – if not the oldest – public houses. The ghost occasionally appears in the bar and has been blamed for tormenting customers.

This spectre was reported several decades ago by the wife of a former licensee and several old customers.

In 1998 *Kent Today* mentioned the haunting, and a former landlord, a Mr Hamill, stated that whilst on holiday a friend looking after the pub had vowed never to stay there again after seeing someone walk across the bar area even though the pub was empty. Mr Hamill said, 'I felt uncomfortable when I first moved in and my dog would run upstairs when I went into the cellar.' Hamill's predecessor called the police one night after hearing noises in the bar when it was closed for business. The *Evening Post* of 4 March 1971 echoed such stories by stating that then owners, a Hetty and Charlie Carpenter, who'd been at the pub two years as of 1971, had also experienced strange noises and ghostly activity.[20]

---

20. Arnold, Neil, *Haunted Rochester*, Kindle edition (The History Press), pp. 75–77.

Right: A grey-robed, monk-like figure emerges through the wall of the bar.

Below: The heart of Rochester is a picturesque centre of the paranormal.

Minor Canon Row, Rochester

In 1723 six houses were built on what is Minor Canon Row (Dickens, in his *Mystery of Edwin Drood*, calls the road Minor Canon Corner and one of his characters, Revd Septimus Crisparkle, was said to reside there). In 1735 No. 7 was added as residence for the cathedral organist. Dame Sybil Thorndike, the celebrated actress, lived in the terrace.

Minor Canon Row is associated with the ghost story of a woman, who, carrying a dead baby, runs from the direction of The Vines. A monk is also said to appear along the road. However, during December 1949, ghost hunter Frederick Sanders recorded in the *Chatham, Rochester & Gillingham News* the 'Grey Phantom of Rochester – Secret of the Old City Gate-Way', mentioning several reports of ghostly footsteps and a darkly adorned spectre roaming the area around Minor Canon Row. Sanders

There are several reports of ghostly footsteps and a darkly adorned spectre roaming the area around Minor Canon Row.

A spectral monk is said to appear along the road.

wrote: I encountered certain people who had sworn with all honesty that they had seen, for a few dreadful seconds, the GREY PHANTOM himself! A cowled figure some had said; a bare-headed, long-cloaked shadow others had explained; a shapeless form, vibrating evil, whispered one palsied old lady ...' Sanders wrote that the legend of the 'grey phantom' dated back further than when the cathedral had a spire. Even so, in typical Sanders fashion, the investigator looked into the reports one moonlit night only to conclude that the ghostly footfalls reported by witnesses were probably nothing more than echoes of their own footsteps. One column of the article speaks of Sander's atmospheric journey into the heart of the haunting. Sanders then, under the heading 'The Grey Phantom Appears', writes, with all the creakiness of a Victorian ghost story, how he encounters his own shadow, cast under a street lamp. However, were these quirky encounters good enough explanations to solve the riddle of the grey phantom? Hardly, but at least Mr Sanders was brave enough to venture into the darkest of Rochester's corners to investigate and experience the strange footfalls along Minor Canon Row, which turned out to be – after much Gothic rambling – a local resident on a nightly stroll!

A Time Slip, Tunbridge Wells

Time slips are occurrences in which a person or people step from their time into another time period. A very unusual paranormal event of this nature took place in Tunbridge Wells on 18 June 1968. I am grateful to Alex Batho of Countryside Books for allowing me to reproduce in full the incident which I have reproduced below, from their book *Supernatural England*:

It was Tunbridge Wells, on the morning of 18 June 1968, and an elderly lady, Mrs Charlotte Warburton, went shopping with her husband in the town. They decided to go their separate ways for a while and to meet up later. Unable to find a particular brand of coffee from her usual grocer she went into a supermarket in Calverley Road. As she entered the shop she saw a small café through an entrance in the left-hand wall. She had never before realised that there was a café there. It was rather old-fashioned with wood panelled walls. There were no windows, and the room was lit by a number of electric bulbs with frosted shades. There was at the time, she thought, nothing especially odd about the scene. 'Two women in rather long dresses were sitting at one table and about half a dozen men, all in dark lounge suits, were sitting at other tables further back in the room,' she said. All the people seemed to be drinking coffee and chatting ... a normal sight for a country town at 11 o'clock in the morning. Mrs Warburton did not stay but she certainly did not recognise anything amiss either then or indeed for several days. Even the rather formal and slightly off-key clothing made no immediate impression on her. Nor did the fact that although the customers were talking there was no noise from them that caused her to question her senses. Nor did she notice that there was no smell of coffee. There is clearly something strange here. Yet without questioning the circumstances in which she found herself, Mrs Warburton blithely left the café and went to meet her husband. And she did not suggest to him that the scene in the café seemed in any way odd. When they came to Tunbridge Wells on their next shopping expedition Mrs Warburton decided to take her husband to the café. Or rather she hoped to take him there. But of course, they never did find the place, though they searched the street up and down. No, they were told in the supermarket, there was no café there. She must be in the wrong building. It was then that they learned about the Kosmos Kinema which had stood on the site of the supermarket. It had had a small café. They were directed to the Tunbridge Wells Constitutional Club where the steward told them that at one time the Constitutional Club had owned the premises adjoining the Kosmos which was now incorporated into the supermarket. The club had had an assembly room in those days and to the rear a small bar with tables for refreshments. Mrs Warburton's description tallied exactly with the club's old refreshment room. The bar, the cinema and the assembly room had all vanished years ago, Mrs Warburton was told. Yet, on 18 June 1968, she had stepped into the past and like others involved in time-slips had accepted without question the place in which she found herself. Retrospective clairvoyance, it is called. Whatever it is, it is mighty odd to contemplate.

Another time-slip incident took place in Kent some years earlier. In 1935 Dr E.G. Moon, a very down-to-earth Scots physician with a practice in Broadstairs, was at Minster in Thanet visiting his patient, Lord Carson, who lived at Cleve Court. After talking to Carson, the doctor left his patient and made his way downstairs into the hallway. His mind was clearly very occupied at the time with the instructions he had given the nurse about the prescription he had left for Carson. At the front door Dr Moon hesitated, wondering whether to go back upstairs to have another word with the nurse.

It was at this point that the doctor noted that his car was no longer where he had left it in the driveway. In fact, it had been parked alongside a thick yew hedge and that too was missing. Even the drive down which he had driven from the main road was now nothing but a muddy track, and a man was coming towards him. The newcomer on the scene, only 30 yards from Dr Moon, was rather oddly dressed, wearing an old-fashioned coat with several capes around the shoulders. And he wore a top hat of the kind seen in the previous century. As he walked he smacked a switch against his riding boots. Over his shoulder he carried a long-barrelled gun. He stared hard at Moon. And the doctor registered the fact that the man coming towards him might have looked more at home in the nineteenth century. Remarkably, Dr Moon seems not at the time to have been either alarmed or even mildly surprised by the changed scenery, by the quite oddly dressed man approaching him or the fact that his car was missing. What preoccupied him was the thought of Lord Carson's prescription. He simply turned away, without any concern, to go back into the house. But he did quite casually take one more look at the scene he was leaving. And now, as if by magic, the car was back where it had been and the yew hedge too. The drive was no longer a muddy track. And the man had also disappeared, back one assumes to the previous century. And it was only now that Dr Moon realised that something odd, something decidedly odd, had occurred. All of this took seconds and so there is every reason to understand why Dr Moon did not immediately go out into the driveway to see where his missing car was. For the same reason it is understandable why he did not speak to the man dressed like a farm bailiff of the past. Dr Moon was drawn into some kind of accepting, hallucinatory state. When he came to – for that seems to be the best way of describing his return to his own time – he described to Lady Carson what he thought had occurred. He was anxious, however, that no word of it should come out in his lifetime for fear that his patients would begin to question his judgement. It was only after his death that the story was revealed. It is difficult to grapple with the notion of time-slips. It may be that all past events are impressed into the fabric of buildings and that in some way and on some occasions, they are released. In other words, what Mrs Warburton and Dr Moon saw were ghosts, but not solely of people but of all of their surroundings. Or did Mrs Warburton and Dr Moon actually return to a real, physical past? Did they turn up as strangers, were they really the interlopers, at somebody else's present? And if so – and this is an intriguing yet unanswerable question - did some people drinking coffee one Saturday morning in a Tunbridge Wells café look up and see Mrs Warburton? Did a man dressed like a farm bailiff, walking towards Cleve Court one day well over a hundred years earlier, see a strangely dressed doctor at the front door of the house? Did the coffee drinkers ever wonder where the elderly lady had so suddenly gone? And did the farm bailiff ask himself how the oddly dressed figure in the doorway had so suddenly disappeared?

Strangely, Tunbridge Wells has thrown up another odd story that may or not have been a time-slip. This tale goes back to some time in the mid-nineteenth century and it took place in the Swan Hotel in The Pantiles. Mrs Nancy Fuller and her young daughter, Naomi, on a first visit to the town, took a room at the top of the hotel, the room now Number 16. As they climbed the stairs to their room the girl's behaviour began to change. She appeared more and more agitated, closing her eyes and whispering to herself. When her mother asked her what was wrong Naomi replied that she recognised the stairway, that she had been there before. Then she came out with the astounding remark that her lover was waiting for her in the room as he had said he always would. When they entered the room the young girl went at once to the corner, calling out 'John' as though to someone standing there waiting. For a few seconds in her mother's eyes she seemed to change, to grow older, and even her clothing was that of an earlier time. The story that Naomi later told her mother was that she had previously lived in this building when it was a privately owned house. This was certainly before 1835 when it became The Swan. In the days when Naomi had lived there it had been known as High House. The young girl went on to explain that she had had a love affair with a man called John, but her father had disapproved, had the young man taken away and had locked her in the room. Alone in the room, aware that she would never again see him, she had conjured up the image of John and holding the hand of her imagined lover, she had jumped to her death from the window. Room 16 is haunted. There are still tales of disarranged bed covers and of chairs being moved, and tapping at the window. Some have claimed to hear the cry 'John' carried on the wind.

But is this an early example of a time-slip? It differs from the other accounts in that Naomi was aware of a past life and her part in it. Some have regarded this story as an instance of reincarnation. Others have seen it as déjà vu. But if reincarnation is the answer, what is it that triggers such an awareness of it? And if déjà vu, how can that come about? Perhaps it is simply a haunting resulting from a young girl's suicide. But the story is so curious that the idea of a time-slip is tempting.

La Casa Vecchia, Tunbridge Wells

La Casa Vecchia, in The Pantiles, is a pleasant bar and restaurant which is allegedly haunted by a grey lady.

Who she is is debatable, but one theory has it that back in the eighteenth century the restaurant was a brothel and the grey lady was the madam of the house. One of the girls working there is said to have gone missing and the legend of the ghost story is that the old woman still looks out of the window, terrifying passers-by, hoping for the young girl to return to the house.

A ghostly old woman allegedly looks out of the window, terrifying passers-by.

The Coach and Horses Passage, Tunbridge Wells

The passage is said to be haunted by a man who hanged himself from a beam after he was robbed, the beam creaking from the weight of an invisible rope. A female ghost is said to haunt Friends Passage. Local people believe the ghost to be the wife of James Friend, once the owner of the Hand and Sceptre Hotel in the nineteenth century.

The passage is said to be haunted by a man who hanged himself from a beam.

Happy Valley, Tunbridge Wells

The Happy Valley area is famous for Sweeps Cave. The story associated with the place is as follows: 'A gypsy was walking through the area late at night when a thunderstorm began. She hurried towards Sweeps Cave where she sheltered from the torrential rain. Once the storm had passed, she continued on her journey and attempted to walk down the hill, via the area where the 105 stairs had previously been covered with mud. This area was notoriously slippery when wet, which, to her dismay, she found out first-hand. She had only just begun her descent down the hill, when she slipped in the mud, and tumbled all the way down the rest of the hill, breaking many bones on her journey to the bottom. Isolated, bleeding and in terrible pain, she realised she was in desperate need of help; when her shouts of help went unanswered, she began dragging herself up the steep slope she had just fallen down. When she was about halfway up, she succumbed to her injuries and died. Her lifeless body was found the morning after; the mark where her shoe had slipped in the mud could still be seen, as could the trail of blood from the bottom of the hill up to where she had managed to pull her injured body.'

Paranormal researcher Alan Tigwell describes an associated event which took place in 2015: 'A woman named Janet was heading down the stairs late one night, taking care as it had rained earlier that evening. She had been to the Beacon pub with her friends and was making her way home via a shortcut through Happy Valley. When she was about a quarter of the way down, she spotted movement further down the hill, just to the right of the steps. It was dark, so she strained to see what it was; she initially thought it was a large animal, but as the shape came closer, she could see it was a woman pulling herself up the hill. Ready to rush to the injured woman's aid, Janet suddenly noticed the woman's movements were strange and there seemed to be a weird black mist spiralling around her; it was as if the woman was gliding her way towards her. Janet explained to me that the woman appeared translucent and the grass around and under the body was not affected by the movements of the woman. When she saw this, Janet turned around and fled back up the stairs and to the Beacon where she told her friends. They immediately went back to the scene to investigate, but the woman could not be found and there was no evidence that the incident had ever taken place.'

Knole, Sevenoaks

Knole is a National Trust property and provides an interesting day out. It has an extensive history and a number of reported phantoms. Richard Sackville, 3rd Earl of Dorset (1598–1624), 'roams the medieval quarters of the house whenever a misfortune is about to befall Knole and has been seen … riding silently on horseback among the leafy shadows …' His portrait hangs in the ballroom. Lady Anne Clifford, daughter of the 3rd Earl of Cumberland (1590–1676), is reported to walk the dark avenue of chestnut and oak trees to the north of Knole's grand gatehouse.

Away from the more formulaic ghost stories, personal encounters are always more interesting and credible. Vic Paler has been visiting Knole for many years with his family. His wife's aunt, Miss Morley, lived and worked at Knole as a National Trust guide from 1946. Paler says he 'can remember walking around the park, but I believe there's a cottage in the grounds which was originally outside

Entrance to Knole House, home of at least three reported phantoms.

Richard Sackville, 3rd Earl of Dorset (1598–1624), 'roams the medieval quarters of the house'.

the grounds, this'd be way back in the English Civil War times, when it was a pub, and there was a public road running by and, this is how the story goes: there was a chap who, fleeing from the Roundheads maybe, had a bag of gold on him, and he, reputedly, was murdered and thrown down the well. I think it then became a gamekeeper's cottage and if you disturbed the area around the well, it would arouse the ghost and there'd be people working out in the garden and they'd look up and there's somebody looking out at them. And when we visited … I can remember the children's faces, you know, because they were … well I suppose they'd just started school, that sort of thing, and the couple who lived there were telling this story and they were going to move because of it … part of the house was modern, added onto the older part of the house; their daughters lived, had their bedrooms, in the old part of the house, and one night they could hear footsteps and this apparition came through and he was floating but there were still footsteps and of course they were screaming for their mum and dad but … I don't know, because the parents didn't wake up? And so they decided to move after that! He was dressed in a long cloak, and, you know, a pointy hat or something.'![21]

21. https://www.knolestories.org.uk/content/working-at-knole/vic-paler

Left: Lady Anne Clifford, daughter of the 3rd Earl of Cumberland (1590–1676), is said to walk the avenue of chestnut and oak trees to the north of Knole's Gatehouse.

Below: Area to the north of Knole's Gatehouse.

The Bull Inn, West Malling

Alan Tigwell reported that he was once 'contacted by the management of The Bull Inn to hear the accounts of paranormal activity taking place on the premises. All the staff had experienced strange events … and thought it would be useful to touch base with someone who investigates paranormal activity. At the time, some of the staff were quite concerned about their experiences and also the stories and tales being told by regulars of the pub, so the management team thought I would be able to provide a certain degree of reassurance. The management advised the inn was built in 1426 and it is believed there are links to the nearby Abbey, with rumours that one of the tunnels from the Abbey is linked to the inn. However, this cannot be proven as the management have attempted to contact the Abbey regarding this, but to no avail. An extension was built in 1995 which doubled the size of the bar and added toilets at the rear. In the cellar, unusual noises have been heard that cannot always be explained (this occurred while the interview was taking place) and when working alone down there, staff have had a feeling of being watched. Equipment failure within the bar has been a regular issue, for instance the soft drinks dispenser has stopped working and upon examination of the equipment and pipes, there appeared to be no fault. When staff tried to use the equipment again, it worked perfectly. The pipes into the bitter barrels have also been pulled above the level of the bitter in the barrel several times, meaning the flow of liquid is interrupted and needs to be physically pushed back down (something else which happened while the interview was taking place). One of the staff members told me she observed through a crack in the floorboards a figure passing by in the cellar, but upon investigation, it was empty. Bangs and scraping (like someone not picking their feet up when they walk) have also been heard. In the restaurant on the ground floor, different witnesses have regularly seen a lady dressed in white walking towards the rear of the room; she is usually seen from an aperture in the bar area. Although the next haunting is not within the pub itself, it can sometimes be observed from the stairway leading to the first floor. When looking out of the window on the stairs, on occasion an old lady laden with a hessian sack can be seen walking up the railway tracks. After a short distance, the lady disappears and there is no evidence of her ever being there. Another tale involving this window is that if you look at the window from outside, you may see the face of a young lady looking back at you. This happened to one staff member on the way into work one day, so they rushed in thinking someone had gained entry to the pub, only to find the place empty except for the manager. They checked the whole of the pub over, but could not explain who the woman was, or where she had gone. Within the living area on the first floor there is what is referred to as "a void" between two walls. A mirror covered the majority of this at the time of the interviews, so it couldn't be examined in detail. Staff advised there is a feeling of oppression when looking into the mirror and they occasionally see a dark shape moving behind them in the reflection. I was told that when the dark shape is witnessed, you can also hear scratching coming from behind the mirror in the void. In what was being used as an office on the first floor, the manager reported he has in the past heard footsteps following him into the office, but when looking behind him, there was no one there. On the first-floor hallway/landing, a lady wearing a long black coat/cloak has been seen walking across the landing towards the bathroom. It is believed that this is the ghost of a nun. The creaking of floorboards could also be heard at the same time. As with similar events within the pub, when checking and looking for the person, no one could be found. In the first-floor bedroom, the manager awoke one night at approximately 4am to hear childish giggling coming from downstairs in the bar area. He immediately went to investigate but when he got to the fourth step from the bottom, the giggling stopped. Undeterred, he continued to investigate but could not find anyone – all the doors were locked and there was no apparent way anyone could exit the building. Each of the two bedrooms upstairs have en-suite bathrooms. In one of them, a staff member told me the bathroom door frequently opens by itself, even though she had ensured it was safely shut. During the interview, I had an opportunity to examine this door. It is not able to open by itself, as the catch is secure and tight. If the catch is not latched correctly, the door does not open or shut on its own accord as the hinges are quite stiff. It appears the regular patrons also have a wealth of knowledge, both about the hauntings and also about the previous residents of The Bull Inn, but it would seem they have resisted providing information to the current management. However, what the staff have gleaned from them is that a previous worker caused himself self-inflicted wounds without knowing what he was doing whilst within the bar area. The patrons indicated to staff there's more to the hauntings that it seems, but were unwilling to discuss or provide any more clarification over what they meant. A few comments have been heard about "something terrible" happening around twenty-five–thirty years ago, but again when questioned they wouldn't give further information. As the interview was ending, one of the staff members mentioned sometimes she felt as though she was being held around the neck in certain areas of the inn. Once this was divulged, all members of staff agreed with her. They also commented that sometimes it felt as though they were being pulled or pushed towards the main doors of the inn.'

Boys Hall, Ashford

The property was originally built in 1616 by the Boys family, who had previously been known as De Bois, having arrived in England from France at the time of the Norman Conquest. The building is now a hotel and restaurant.

In 2007, the *Most Haunted* team visited Boys Hall. They reported activity including a ghost of a dog, things flying around, crying children, doors flying open, locks rattling, poltergeist activity in the kitchen and objects being thrown.

The established ghost stories are that over 200 years ago 'the son of the house was betrothed to one Ellen Scott who, at a party at the house, met and fell in love with a handsome individual named Tracey, much to the annoyance and indeed blind anger of her fiancé who insisted on the agreed marriage taking place. Meanwhile the mysterious Tracey completely disappeared and during the years that followed Ellen and her husband spent a lot of time abroad where she eventually became a widow. One night the then occupants of Boys Hall were startled to hear a loud knocking on the front door of the house, accompanied by pitiful moaning noises and heart-rending sobs. On opening the door they were astonished to find Ellen, distraught, clad only in a thin white dress and mumbling about still looking for her true love, Tracey… She stumbled into the house, staggered up the stairs and disappeared into a bedroom. The occupants looked at one another: surely the poor girl had lost her reason –suddenly screams echoed through the great house and they rushed upstairs to find Ellen ranting and raving beside a secret hiding place she had exposed by removing some floorboards. Inside were the remains of a human dressed as Tracey had once been dressed . . . and a bullet dropped from the skull when it was moved. Before anyone could stop her Ellen had rushed to a window and jumped to her death. At a subsequent inquest on the two bodies the startling announcement was made that the remains of Tracey were those of a female! Small wonder that odd happenings have been reported from time to time at Boys Hall. A figure in white gliding noiselessly in one of the bedrooms; footsteps sounding along a corridor and down a stairway; inexplicable sounds emanating from empty rooms; a padding sound; a crashing and hammering noise; sounds of sighing and heavy breathing; and occasional "touchings" in one of the upper rooms. The haunting of Boys Hall is as much a mystery as the history of the place itself and those who once lived there.'[22]

As a rider there's an interesting comment on TripAdvisor for Boys Hall when in 23 October 2019 Suzanne C wrote, 'my partner and myself came for an overnight stay to celebrate a special birthday. The hotel itself and food were amazing and our room unbelievable. I have always been a spiritual type of person my partner used to be a huge sceptic. I felt a presence in the room from the time we went into our room to go

---

22. Underwood, Peter. Ghosts of Kent: Illustrated Edition.

This much-haunted building is alleged to include a figure in white gliding noiselessly in one of the bedrooms and footsteps sounding along a corridor.

to bed, then the banging started. The room got colder until we could see our breath. We huddled up to keep warm but were kept awake most of the night with whispering noises, banging on walls and other strange noises. I always thought I'd love to stay somewhere haunted but I was terrified. My husband is no longer sceptical. But a totally beautiful old Manor house.'

Acknowledgements

I would like to thank the following for their encouragement and help in the writing of this book.

Adele Newman, Tina Jacobs, Alan Tigwell, and the staff at Fort Amherst for their fascinating private tour of the tunnels.